D.C. WINTER

THE LAST-MINUTE PREPPER

48 Hours to Ready When Disaster Strikes

**WINTERS HERE
PRESS**

To the Doomsday Clock timekeepers. Your job is done.

You've got 48 hours. Starting now.

Contents

Foreword

No time to waste. Read and get moving.

Preface

We are past the time is nigh. It's here.

Acknowledgments

I'd like to give thanks to all of the staff at Winters Here Press who made this book even better than my first, *The Progressive's 2025 Guide to Prepping.*

1

So You Waited Until the Last Minute

You're holding this book because the world as you knew it is ending or has already ended. The power grid might be flickering. Your phone notifications may have delivered their final, ominous alerts before going silent. *Bricked.* Perhaps you've spotted unfamiliar military vehicles rolling through your neighborhood, or you've noticed an eerie absence of air traffic overhead. Maybe the financial markets have collapsed, a pandemic has exploded beyond containment, or that distant rumbling isn't thunder.

And here you are, completely unprepared.

First, take a deep breath. Now take another one. Good.

My name is D.C. Winter. For over thirty years, I've been telling anyone who would listen (and plenty who wouldn't) that this day was coming. I've written books, hosted seminars, and built communities dedicated to preparation for societal disruption. I've stockpiled supplies, honed skills, and constructed self-sufficient systems while my neighbors planned vacations and debated kitchen renovations.

So yes, this is technically the part where I get to say "I told you so."

But that wouldn't help either of us right now, would it?

Instead, I'm going to tell you something that might surprise you: You're not as screwed as you think you are.

The "I Told You So" You Actually Need Right Now

Let's dispense with the prepper superiority complex that pervades too many survival guides. Yes, those of us who prepared have advantages. We have supplies. We have plans. We have practiced. But here's what I've learned after decades of preparation: the human capacity for adaptation is remarkable, and it's your greatest asset right now.

The apocalypse doesn't care if you believed in it before it arrived. It's here now, and your past skepticism is irrelevant to your future survival. What matters is what you do in the next 48 hours, and that's where this book comes in.

Truth be told, many "prepared" individuals are operating on outdated assumptions, rigid protocols that may not fit the actual crisis at hand, or skills that haven't been truly tested. Your adaptability—your ability to assess, learn, and implement quickly without the baggage of preconceived notions—might actually serve you better than someone who's been rehearsing for the wrong apocalypse.

You have one tremendous advantage: urgency. Nothing focuses the mind like necessity. The prepared have often grown comfortable in their preparations; you don't have that luxury. Your learning curve will be steep, but your motivation is pure. Use it.

What you're reading isn't a watered-down version of survival information. It's concentrated and distilled to its most essential elements. I won't waste your time with philosophical musings on the collapse of civilization or detailed explanations of why certain strategies work. You need actionable intelligence, and you need it now.

Consider this your field commission to the ranks of the prepared. Welcome to the last-minute survival crash course.

How to Use This Book When Time Is Your Scarcest Resource

This book assumes two things: you have very little time, and you have very few specialized supplies. Every recommendation takes these limitations into account.

First, understand that this is not a book you read from cover to cover. It's an emergency response manual designed for immediate implementation. Here's how to use it effectively:

1. Scan the chapter titles and identify your most pressing vulnerabilities. Are you in a water-insecure location? Start with Chapter 1. Facing immediate security threats? Jump to Chapter 6. Don't worry about reading in order.

2. Focus on what you can accomplish in your specific environment. Urban apartment dwellers will implement different strategies than suburban homeowners or rural residents. Look for the environment-specific notations throughout the text.

3. Implement as you read. This book is designed to be read in motion. *Get moving!* Read a section, implement its advice immediately, then return for the next section. Have household members implement different sections simultaneously if possible.

4. Use the time indicators. Throughout the text, you'll find time estimates for various tasks. These aren't arbitrary— they're based on real-world testing with unprepared individuals. Trust them, and prioritize accordingly.

5. Improvise with what you have. Every recommendation includes alternatives using common household items. The

3

"ideal" solution is less important than an adequate solution implemented immediately.

Time compression is your reality now. In normal circumstances, you might take weeks to research water filtration systems, comparing features and reading reviews. Now, you need to create a water filtration system in the next hour using materials in your home. This book will show you how.

Remember: in a crisis, adequate action now always beats perfect action later. The 80/20 rule is your new best friend—in almost any preparedness category, 80% of the benefit comes from the first 20% of the effort. We're going to focus relentlessly on that critical 20%.

The 48-Hour Mindset: Focused, Efficient, and No Room for Panic

The next 48 hours will determine much of your long-term survival prospects. This compressed timeframe requires a specific mindset—one that balances urgency with methodical action.

First, accept your new reality completely. Denial is a luxury you cannot afford. Whatever you thought would happen tomorrow—work meetings, social gatherings, routine activities—is now irrelevant. Your only priority is stabilizing your situation in preparation for extended disruption.

Second, embrace radical prioritization. In normal times, your attention might be divided among dozens of concerns. Now, you'll be focusing on the survival hierarchy:

Water
Security
Shelter/Warmth
Food
Medical

Communication

Everything else

Notice that food is fourth on this list, not second. This often surprises people, but you can survive weeks without food. You cannot survive days without water or security. Trust the hierarchy—it's built on the physiological realities of human survival, not comfort preferences.

Third, adopt tactical tunnel vision. For the next 48 hours, every action should directly support your survival objectives. This isn't the time for long-term planning, emotional processing, or complex decision-making beyond immediate needs. Stay ruthlessly practical.

Fourth, recognize that sleep remains essential. The survival mindset often pushes people toward sleep deprivation in the rush to prepare. This is a critical mistake. Cognitive impairment from lack of sleep will compromise your decision-making precisely when clear thinking is most valuable. Schedule at least two 4-hour sleep blocks within your 48-hour preparation window.

Fifth, control your information intake. In a crisis, information becomes both extremely valuable and dangerously unreliable. Establish specific times to gather intelligence, then focus on implementation. Constant monitoring of emergency broadcasts or social media will paralyze you with information overload.

Finally, understand that panic is not just an emotional state—it's a resource allocation problem. When you panic, your body redirects blood flow away from your prefrontal cortex (where strategic thinking happens) and into your limbic system and extremities (preparing you to fight or flee). This physiological response served our ancestors well when facing predators, but it directly inhibits the complex thinking needed for modern crisis response.

The antidote to panic is not calm—it's directed action. This book provides that direction. When you feel panic rising, don't fight the emotion directly. Instead, redirect it into the next concrete task. Your physiology will follow your actions.

You have exactly 48 hours to establish baseline preparedness. Not 47. Not 49. This arbitrary deadline serves a psychological purpose: it creates urgency without inducing paralysis. The timeline is tight but achievable—if you start now.

How to Use the Quick-Start Guides Effectively

Each chapter in this book concludes with a single-page quick-start guide—a condensed, visually organized summary of the most critical information. These are not afterthoughts or supplemental material; they are the tactical heart of this book.

The quick-start guides follow a consistent format designed for immediate implementation:

The Priority Matrix at the top ranks actions by both impact and urgency. Always start with the high-impact, high-urgency quadrant and work clockwise. This visual triage tool prevents you from wasting precious time on low-value activities, no matter how tempting they might be.

The Time Block Allocations divide your available time into critical task categories. These are not suggestions—they're prescriptive time management protocols tested in actual crisis environments. If the guide allocates 20 minutes to water container preparation, spend exactly 20 minutes on this task, then move on regardless of completion level. Perfect is the enemy of done.

The Resource Maps identify common household items that can serve survival functions. Your home contains dozens of survival tools disguised as everyday objects. These maps will help you identify and repurpose them quickly.

The Decision Trees provide binary pathways through complex situational variables. Crisis decision-making must be simplified to be effective. These decision trees distill complex situational factors into clear action pathways.

The Completion Checklist at the bottom of each guide provides verification that you've implemented the essential elements. In crisis conditions, memory and attention become compromised. The checklist ensures nothing critical falls through the cracks.

To use these guides effectively:

1. Make multiple copies immediately. If possible, laminate at least one copy or place it in a waterproof container. Digital copies are useful but cannot be your only version.

2. Assign a guide administrator. If you're not alone, designate someone to manage the implementation of each guide, tracking progress and ensuring completion.

3. Use visual marking systems. As you implement each element, mark it visibly. This creates a visual progress map that motivates continued action and prevents redundant effort.

4. Set timers for each section. Temporal discipline is essential when resources are limited. Use your phone timer while it still functions, or any available timepiece.

5. Verbalize completions. The act of verbally confirming completed tasks helps cement them in memory and reduces anxiety about forgotten elements.

These quick-start guides distill decades of survival knowledge and crisis response experience into actionable protocols that anyone can implement, regardless of prior preparation. *Anyone!* Even you. They are designed to be intuitive even under extreme stress, when cognitive function may be impaired by fear, fatigue, or overwhelm.

Remember: these guides were developed and field-tested by survivors of actual societal disruptions—from natural disasters to political collapse to technological failures. They represent not just theoretical best practices but proven survival protocols.

Final Thoughts Before You Begin

Perhaps you're feeling a twinge of shame right now. Maybe you're remembering conversations where you dismissed preparation as paranoia, or times you prioritized comfort over resilience. Perhaps you're thinking of the prepper in your life whose warnings you ignored.

Let it go. *All of it.*

Survival is forward-facing. What matters isn't what you did or didn't do before the crisis—it's what you do now. History is filled with unlikely survivors who had no business making it through their particular apocalypse, yet somehow did. Their secret wasn't prior preparation but present adaptation.

You are now officially a prepper. The fact that you began thirty seconds ago is irrelevant.

In the pages that follow, you'll find specific, actionable protocols for establishing baseline survival capability within 48 hours. Some will seem counterintuitive. Others will challenge conventional wisdom. All have been validated in actual crisis environments with unprepared individuals.

Trust the process. Execute with precision. Adapt to your specific circumstances.

The world as you knew it has ended. Your survival journey is just beginning. Turn the page, and let's get to work.

You've got 47 hours and 59 minutes left.

2

Water - Your First 48 Hours of Survival

Why Water Comes First: The Rule of Threes

When society collapses, your survival priorities aren't what you think they are. Your instinct will be to panic about food, weapons, or communications. Resist this impulse. Water comes first, and I'm going to tell you exactly why.

The *Rule of Threes* is the foundational principle of survival prioritization. It states:

- You can survive 3 minutes without air
- You can survive 3 hours without shelter (in extreme conditions)
- You can survive 3 days without water
- You can survive 3 weeks without food

Notice where water falls on this hierarchy. While you won't die immediately without it, your decision-making capacity will begin to deteriorate within 24 hours of dehydration. By 36 hours, your physical capabilities will be significantly compromised. By 48 hours, you'll be entering a crisis state where rational thought becomes nearly impossible.

Here's what dehydration does to your body during a crisis:
- **1% dehydration**: Thirst begins, cognitive performance degrades subtly
- **2% dehydration**: Clear thinking becomes difficult, physical performance drops by 20%
- **4% dehydration**: Physical capacity decreases by 40%, nausea begins
- **6% dehydration**: Disorientation, heat regulation fails
- **10% dehydration**: Circulatory collapse becomes imminent, survival unlikely

The cruel irony is that the more dehydrated you become, the less capable you are of solving your water problem. This creates a downward spiral that has killed countless people in disaster scenarios.

Water is also unique among survival resources because:
1. **It cannot be improvised or substituted effectively**
2. **It's required in relatively large quantities daily**
3. **It's heavy and difficult to transport**
4. **Contaminated water creates secondary survival threats**

Unlike food energy, which your body can extract from a vast array of substances, your body has no mechanism to extract water from non-liquid sources in meaningful quantities. The water you consume must be actual water.

This is why securing your water supply isn't just your first priority—it's the foundation upon which all your other survival activities will rest. In a crisis scenario, water truly is life.

Immediate Water Sourcing from Your Home Environment
Your home contains more available water than you realize.
We're going to identify and secure it immediately.

Trapped Water in Your Plumbing
The moment you suspect infrastructure failure, do the following:

1. Fill your bathtub(s) and sinks. Do this before pressure drops in municipal systems. A standard bathtub holds 30-50 gallons—potentially a week's worth of water for one person.

2. Turn off the main water valve to your home. This prevents contamination from backing up into your home system when municipal pressure fails. The valve is typically located where the main water line enters your home, often in a basement, crawlspace, or near your water heater.

3. Drain the water from your home's pipes by opening the highest faucet in your home (typically an upstairs bathroom) and then opening the lowest faucet (typically in a basement or first floor). This creates a siphon effect, allowing gravity to drain water into containers. This can yield 30+ gallons in an average home.

4. Access your water heater. It contains 40-80 gallons of preheated, relatively clean water. To access it:
- Turn off the power/gas to the water heater first
- Locate the drain valve near the bottom of the tank
- Attach a garden hose or open the valve directly into containers
- Open a hot water faucet somewhere in the house to break the vacuum seal

5. Don't forget the toilet tanks (not bowls). Each tank contains 1.5-3 gallons of clean water. Remove the lid and scoop it out with a cup. The water in toilet tanks is the same clean water that flows from your taps.

Hidden Water Sources

Plants and natural materials in your home can yield unexpected water in dire circumstances. Houseplants store significant moisture—their soil can be wrapped in cloth and squeezed, yielding small amounts of filtered water. Some succulents and cacti contain water that can be extracted by carefully cutting and pressing the flesh. Even fresh fruits and vegetables in your refrigerator hold valuable water content— a medium cucumber is approximately 95% water and can be pressed to extract liquid in emergencies. Your home's structure itself may provide emergency water opportunities. HVAC systems often produce condensation, particularly in humid environments. Air conditioning units can generate several gallons of condensate daily during operation; capture this before power loss. Dehumidifiers similarly collect water that, while not potable without treatment, can be purified for consumption. In cooler climates, frozen pipes that thaw may release trapped water—place containers to capture this resource. Even morning dew collecting on windows, metal surfaces, or plastic sheeting can be harvested by wiping with clean cloths and wringing into containers.

Vehicles parked on your property represent another overlooked water resource. Automobile air conditioning systems produce condensation that drips beneath the vehicle—place a clean container under the drainage point after operation. Windshield washer fluid reservoirs typically hold 1-3 gallons of liquid; while the commercial fluid is toxic, an empty reservoir can store potable water. The engine cooling system contains several gallons of liquid but should only be considered for non-consumption purposes due to toxic additives. Even a vehicle's

13

fuel tank, once emptied of fuel and thoroughly cleaned, can serve as a large-capacity water storage container in extended emergencies—though this should be considered an absolute last resort requiring extensive preparation.

Look for these often-overlooked water sources in a typical home:

1. Ice maker and ice cube trays in your freezer: Melt immediately before power loss makes them inaccessible.

2. Canned vegetables and fruits: The liquid can be consumed and typically contains a small amount of the nutrients from the food.

3. Waterbed: If you have one, it contains 150-200 gallons. Use this water for non-consumption purposes unless you have confirmed ability to purify it properly.

4. Radiators and water-cooling systems: Consider these contaminated; use for sanitation only.

5. Swimming pools and aquariums: Pool water contains chemicals that make it a last resort for drinking, but viable when properly treated. Aquarium water can be purified but contains high levels of nitrogen waste.

6. Exterior drainage: Your home's rain gutters and downspouts can be modified to catch rainfall. Deploy containers immediately if precipitation is imminent.

Assessing Local Water Sources

Within 24 hours, you need to identify sustainable water sources beyond your home's immediate supply.

Urban infrastructure often contains overlooked water repositories ideal for emergency collection. Abandoned or damaged buildings frequently have intact plumbing systems with significant trapped water—access basements where water has collected from broken pipes or utility rooms housing multiple water heaters. Municipal parks typically feature irrigation systems with underground access points containing several gallons of relatively clean water. Fire hydrants, while technically illegal to access without authorization, can be operated with specialized tools in genuine survival scenarios and deliver hundreds of gallons quickly. Construction sites often maintain water tanks for mixing concrete and dust suppression; these unmarked containers may hold 250-1,000+ gallons of untreated but usable water.

Transportation infrastructure presents unique water harvesting opportunities. Highway underpasses channel and collect rainwater, often creating persistent puddles that can be filtered for emergency use. Railroad corridors frequently incorporate drainage systems that funnel rainwater to collection points, offering relatively clean water compared to standing surface water. Abandoned or damaged vehicles, particularly commercial trucks, buses, and recreational vehicles, contain multiple water systems—cooling systems, drinking water tanks, and onboard plumbing may yield 5-100 gallons depending on the vehicle type. Commercial properties with irrigation systems often maintain 500+ gallon cisterns that continue functioning briefly during power outages due to residual pressure, providing a significant but time-sensitive collection opportunity immediately following infrastructure failure.

Sustainable water sources may also include:

1. **Natural sources: Streams, rivers, ponds, lakes within walking distance**
    - Flowing water is generally preferable to standing water
    - Moving deeper into watershed areas improves water quality
    - Upstream is preferred to downstream when population

centers are involved

2. Community sources: Public pools, decorative fountains, water towers

- Public pools contain approximately 15,000-60,000 gallons and chlorine levels will make them safer than other standing water in the short term
- Decorative water features often have minimal chemical treatment and should be considered contaminated
- Water towers typically contain 150,000-300,000 gallons but accessing them requires specialized knowledge

3. Commercial sources: Office water coolers, vending machines, fire sprinkler systems

- Office buildings often have multiple 5-gallon water cooler bottles
- Beverage vending machines typically contain 5-20 gallons of filtered water
- Sprinkler systems contain stagnant, non-potable water that requires extensive treatment

4. Industrial sources: These are high-risk, last resort options that require substantial treatment and should only be considered in extreme circumstances.

Remember: Visibility is not a reliable indicator of water quality. Clear water can contain lethal pathogens; cloudy water may be made potable with proper treatment.

Emergency Purification Methods with Household Items

Not all water is created equal. Drinking contaminated water can incapacitate you through bacterial, viral, or parasitic infection within hours—defeating the purpose of securing water in the first place. Here are your purification options using common household items:

Heat Purification

Boiling is the most reliable method available without specialized equipment:

1. Bring water to a rolling boil for a minimum of 1 minute (3 minutes at elevations above 6,500 feet)

2. Allow to cool naturally; do not add ice to speed cooling

3. Pour the water back and forth between two clean containers to improve taste by re-oxygenating it

If power is unavailable, use:
- Gas stove/grill
- Fire pit with a metal container
- Solar methods: A glass container in direct sunlight reaches pasteurization temperatures (149°F/65°C) within 3-5 hours, killing most pathogens

Chemical Purification
Household chemicals can disinfect water when used correctly:

1. **Unscented household bleach (5.25-8.25% sodium hypochlorite):**
- 2 drops per quart for clear water
- 4 drops per quart for cloudy water
- Stir and let stand for 30 minutes
- Should have a slight chlorine odor; if not, repeat dosage
- **WARNING**: *Bleach effectiveness degrades over time, in half after 6 months.*

2. Tincture of iodine (2%):
   - 5 drops per quart for clear water
   - 10 drops per quart for cloudy water
   - Stir and let stand for 30 minutes
   - NOT recommended for pregnant women, those with thyroid issues, or for long-term

3. Hydrogen peroxide (3%):
   - A last resort option
   - 25 drops per quart
   - Stir and let stand for 30 minutes

4. Pool shock (calcium hypochlorite, 65-75%):
   - Create a chlorine solution by dissolving 1 heaping teaspoon in 2 gallons of water
   - Use this as a disinfecting stock solution, adding 1 part stock solution to 100 parts water
   - Let stand for 30 minutes
   - **WARNING**: *Highly caustic in concentrated form; handle with extreme care*

Filtration Methods
   Improvised filtration reduces particulates and some contaminants but does not eliminate all pathogens:

1. Multilayer cloth filtration:
   - Layer multiple clean cotton fabrics (t-shirts, pillowcases)
   - Pour water through repeatedly, replacing or cleaning filters as they clog
   - This removes visible particulates only; further treatment is required

2. Homemade charcoal filter:
 - Layer a container with gravel, sand, and crushed charcoal
(from a wood fire, not briquettes)
 - Pour water through multiple times
 - Follow with chemical or heat treatment

3. Improvised ceramic filter:
 - Terracotta flower pots with the drainage holes plugged can
act as crude filters
 - Results vary significantly; always follow with chemical or
heat treatment
 Remember: All improvised filtration methods should be followed by chemical or heat treatment. Filtering simply prepares
water for final purification.

Storage Solutions Using Found Containers
 Once you've sourced and purified water, proper storage becomes critical. Water improperly stored can become contaminated, rendering your previous efforts useless. Here's how to
use what you have:

Primary Storage Options
 Assess your home for these containers, listed in order of
preference:
 1. Purpose-built water containers:
 - Water dispenser bottles (3-5 gallons)
 - Camping jugs
 - Hydration bladders from hiking gear
 - Emergency water bags/pouches

2. Food-grade plastic containers:
 - Soda/juice bottles (thoroughly rinsed)

- Milk jugs (less ideal due to fat residue that promotes bacterial growth)
- Large food service containers (pickle buckets, bulk ingredient containers)
- Water bottles

3. Glass containers:
- Juice/beverage bottles
- Preserving/canning jars
- Beverage pitchers

Unsuitable Containers (Emergency Use Only)
Avoid these if possible, but in true emergencies when no alternatives exist:

1. Non-food-grade containers:
- Household chemical bottles (bleach, detergent)
- Automotive fluid containers
- Must be thoroughly cleaned with soap, rinsed repeatedly
- Use these for non-consumption purposes whenever possible (sanitation, washing)

2. Collapsible containers:
- Bathtubs
- Sinks
- Washing machines
- Line with clean plastic sheeting if available
- Cover to prevent contamination and evaporation

Improvised Large-Scale Storage
For storing larger quantities when conventional containers

are unavailable:

1. Sheet method:
- Line a depression in the ground with clean plastic sheeting
- Create a shallow basin to collect and hold water
- Cover with another sheet to prevent contamination and slow evaporation
- Best for temporary storage of non-drinking water

2. Furniture conversion:
- Dressers with drawers removed and lined with plastic sheeting
- Bookshelves laid on their backs, lined with plastic
- Reinforced cardboard boxes lined with garbage bags (short-term only)

3. Vehicle components:
- Vehicle fuel tanks (emptied and cleaned) can store 12-20 gallons
- *EXTREME EMERGENCY ONLY: requires extensive cleaning and treatment*

Storage Principles

Follow these principles regardless of the containers you use:

1. Rotation: Use older stored water first; monitor and replace regularly

2. Distribution: Don't keep all water in one location

3. Security: Hide a portion of your supply from casual observation

4. Temperature: Store in cool, dark locations whenever possible to limit algae growth

5. Contamination prevention: Ensure all containers are sealed

6. Documentation: Mark containers with date of filling and purification method used

How to Calculate Your Water Needs

Understanding your precise water requirements allows for effective rationing and prevents both dangerous dehydration and wasteful overconsumption.

Baseline Requirements

The absolute minimum survival water requirements are:

- 1 gallon (3.78 liters) per person per day in moderate climates and minimal activity
    - This includes:
    - 2 quarts (1.9 liters) for drinking
    - 1 quart (0.95 liters) for food preparation
    - 1 quart (0.95 liters) for hygiene

This is a **SURVIVAL** minimum, not a comfort minimum. Your body will experience mild dehydration even at this level.

Adjustment Factors

Multiply your baseline by these factors for accurate requirements:

1. Climate factors:
    - Hot environment (85°F+/29°C+): Multiply by 1.5
    - Very hot environment (100°F+/38°C+): Multiply by 2
    - Cold environment (below 32°F/0°C): Multiply by 1.25

2. Activity level factors:
    - Moderate activity (securing shelter, collecting resources): Multiply by 1.25

- Heavy activity (traveling on foot, carrying loads): Multiply by 1.5
- Intense activity (running, combat, heavy labor): Multiply by 2

3. Health condition factors:
- Pregnancy/nursing: Multiply by 1.5
- Illness with fever: Multiply by 1.5
- Illness with vomiting/diarrhea: Multiply by 2 (critical to replace lost fluids)

4. Age factors:
- Children under 8: Multiply by 0.75
- Elderly (over 65): Multiply by 1.25

These factors are cumulative. Example: A pregnant woman performing moderate activity in hot weather would calculate: 1 gallon × 1.5 (pregnancy) × 1.25 (moderate activity) × 1.5 (hot environment) = 2.8 gallons per day.

Strategic Water Budgeting

When supplies are limited, allocate your water strategically:

1. Core hydration: 60% of your supply
- This is non-negotiable; without this, all other activities become impossible

2. Food preparation: 20% of your supply
- Can be reduced by choosing foods that require no preparation
- Water used for rehydrating or cooking food provides both hydration and nutrition

3. Hygiene: 15% of your supply
- Prioritize hand cleaning before food handling

- Focus on wound care to prevent infection
- Use same water for multiple hygiene purposes when possible (e.g., hand washing water can be reused for wiping surfaces)
  4. Reserve/contingency: 5% of your supply
- Maintain a small reserve for unexpected needs
- Distribute this throughout your storage locations

Monitoring Hydration Status

Learn to assess your hydration level accurately:
  1. Urine color chart:
- Clear to light yellow: Well-hydrated
- Medium yellow: Mild dehydration
- Dark yellow to amber: Significant dehydration
- Orange to brown: Severe dehydration; immediate action required

2. Physical indicators:
- Pinch skin on back of hand; if it doesn't quickly return to normal, you're dehydrated
- Dry mouth and lips
- Reduced tear production
- Headache and dizziness
- Fatigue and irritability

3. Performance indicators:
- Difficulty concentrating on simple tasks
- Slowed reaction time
- Physical weakness
- These often occur before you recognize thirst

Making water calculations a habit creates awareness that prevents both dangerous dehydration and wasteful overconsumption. In survival situations, this awareness may determine your outcome.

WATER PRIORITY TIME BLOCK ALLOCATIONS

Survival depends not just on what you do, but when you do it. The following time blocks represent your operational battle plan for water security during the critical 48-hour window. These aren't suggestions—they're tactical imperatives based on disaster response patterns from multiple collapse scenarios. The timing is precisely calibrated to maximize resource acquisition before competition increases and to ensure basic hydration needs remain met throughout the initial crisis period. Follow this schedule with military precision, using timers when available. Each minute spent on lower-priority tasks directly compromises your water security position. These allocations account for practical execution time, including interruptions and complications typically encountered during infrastructure failure. Commit this sequence to memory immediately:

First Hour Focus (60 minutes):
   - Container collection and preparation: 10 minutes
   - Filling bathtubs and sinks: 10 minutes
   - Securing water main and system: 5 minutes
   - Calculating water requirements: 5 minutes
   - Initial container filling: 20 minutes
   - Organization and planning: 10 minutes

Immediate Follow-up (120 minutes):
   - Water heater drainage: 30 minutes
   - Pipe water extraction: 30 minutes

- Alternative source collection: 30 minutes
- Initial purification batch: 30 minutes

RESOURCE MAP: HOUSEHOLD WATER SOURCES

Primary Sources (High Volume):
- Water heater: 40-80 gallons
- Bathtub: 30-50 gallons per tub
- Pipes: 30+ gallons after main shut-off
- Hot water baseboard heating system: 5-15 gallons

Secondary Sources (Medium Volume):
- Toilet tanks: 1.5-3 gallons each
- Refrigerator water dispenser line: 0.5-1 gallon
- Waterbed: 150-200 gallons (requires extensive purification)
- Fish tanks: Varies (requires extensive purification)

Tertiary Sources (Low Volume):
- Ice cube trays: 0.5-1 quart
- Canned goods liquid: 0.25-0.5 cup per can
- Bottled beverages: Varies
- Household plants: Minimal emergency source

DECISION TREE: WATER PURIFICATION METHOD SELECTION
START HERE

▼

Is heat available? ————— YES ———► BOIL WATER (1 min, 3 min at high elevation)

NO

▼

Have bleach/iodine? ————— YES ———► USE CHEMI-
CALS

  | |

  | ▼

  | Clear water? ——— YES ———► 2 drops bleach per quart

  | NO |

▼ | NO

▼

Have sun exposure? ————— YES ———► 4 drops bleach
per quart

  |

  | NO

▼

LAST RESORT: Filter through cloth + let settle 12+ hours

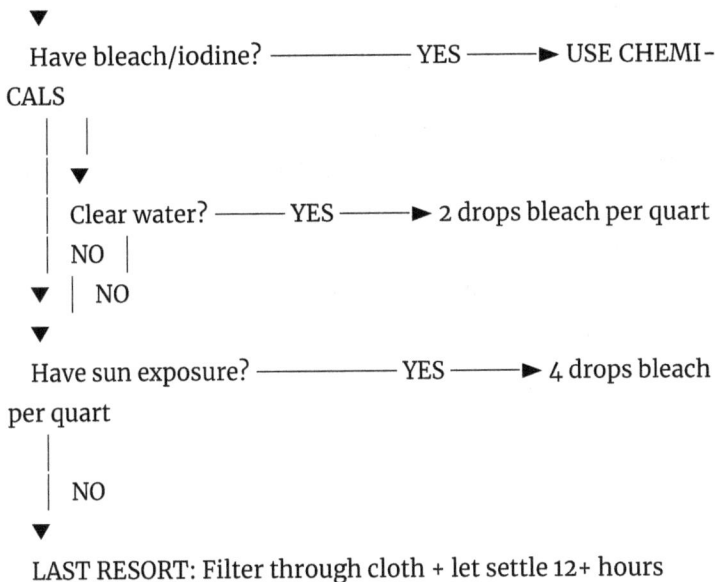

COMPLETION CHECKLIST

Water Collection Complete When:
- ☐ All immediately accessible water has been collected
- ☐ All improvised containers have been deployed
- ☐ A minimum of 3 gallons per person has been secured
- ☐ Water sources have been prioritized by quality

Water Purification Complete When:
- ☐ Primary purification method is functional
- ☐ Backup purification method is identified
- ☐ Test purification has been verified
- ☐ All collected water has been treated or scheduled for treatment

Water Storage Complete When:

- ☐ All containers are properly sealed
- ☐ Water is stored in cool, dark locations where possible
- ☐ Storage locations are distributed for security
- ☐ All containers are labeled with date and purification status

Water System Complete When:

- ☐ Daily rationing plan is established
- ☐ Water usage priorities are communicated to all group members
- ☐ Conservation methods are implemented
- ☐ Ongoing collection strategy is operational

3

What Food to Grab When the Shelves Are Emptying

In the world of survival priorities, food comes fourth, not first. But don't tell your panicking brain that—it's hardwired to focus on food scarcity with an intensity that defies logic. Ever notice how crowded grocery stores get before a minor snowstorm? *There's no milk left!* Now little inconvenience multiply that by apocalypse. When society begins to unravel, people don't rationally fill their carts with calculated nutrition—they grab whatever triggers their primitive brains' survival instincts, usually high-carb comfort foods with terrible shelf lives and minimal nutritional value.

You're going to be smarter than that. Much smarter.

I've witnessed food riots on three continents. I've seen suburban professionals nearly stab each other over the last box of Pop-Tarts. *That strawberry frosted is mine!* I've watched otherwise reasonable people fill shopping carts with perishable luxury items while ignoring the beans and rice that might actually keep them alive. The psychology of panic shopping is fascinating—and completely predictable.

Your advantage? You're reading this while they're still watching cat videos or arguing about politics on social media. By the time they realize what's happening, you'll already have executed a strategic acquisition plan that puts you weeks or months ahead of the curve.

Let's get to work.

Strategic Shopping When Everyone Else Is Panicking

When disaster strikes, your local grocery store transforms from a mundane retail environment into a psychological battlefield. Understanding the predictable patterns of panic shopping gives you a critical tactical advantage.

First, recognize the psychology of the panicked shopper. They'll focus on:

- Familiar comfort foods (often with poor nutritional profiles)
- Pre-packaged, ready-to-eat items (regardless of nutritional value)
- Obvious survival foods that have entered popular culture (water, bread, milk)
- Items in the front and at eye level (exactly where stores place their lowest-value, highest-margin products)

Your counter-strategy exploits these predictable behaviors. While the masses fight over the last loaf of bread, you'll be efficiently collecting the overlooked essentials that actually matter.

Timing Is Everything

The moment you suspect a crisis is developing, execute your shopping run immediately. Every hour you delay exponentially increases both the competition and the likelihood of restrictions. Here's your timing strategy:

1. **Go NOW, not later.** The difference between shopping three hours before the general public recognizes a crisis and three hours after can be the difference between a full cart and empty shelves.
2. **Shop during off-peak hours.** If possible, shop during the least busy times—typically early morning (4-6 AM) or late evening (10 PM-midnight). During a developing crisis, 24-hour stores offer a critical advantage.
3. **Target the right stores.** In the initial phase of a crisis:

- Avoid obvious destinations like Walmart, Costco, and major grocery chains
- Prioritize ethnic grocery stores (Latin, Asian, Middle Eastern markets often have excellent bulk staples)
- Discount grocery outlets (Aldi, Lidl, etc.)
- Drug stores and convenience stores (higher prices but overlooked by many panicked shoppers)
- Restaurant supply stores (often open to the public and stocked with large-quantity staples)
- Hardware stores (which often have camping food sections untouched during food panics)

1. **Multi-store strategy.** Never put all your acquisition hopes in one location. Plan a circuit of three-to-five stores in decreasing order of priority. Spend no more than 20 minutes in each location.

Tactical Shopping Approach

Once inside, your approach should be methodical, not frantic. You're not foraging—you're executing a precision operation:

1. **Enter with a list, not an idea.** The attached quick-start guide provides your framework. Modify only if you encounter unexpected opportunities.
2. **Shop the perimeter last, not first.** Contrary to normal healthy shopping advice, during a crisis, start with center aisles containing shelf-stable items. The perimeter (produce, meat, dairy) contains higher nutritional value but lower shelf stability. Grab these only after securing your non-perishable foundation.
3. **Think below and above.** Most shoppers grab products at eye level. Consistently look at the highest and lowest shelves, where the most cost-effective options often hide.
4. **Skip the obvious.** If you see a crowd gathering in one section, skip it entirely on your first pass. Return only after completing your primary list. The time you waste competing for the last can of tuna exceeds the value of that protein.
5. **Stay silent, look average.** Do not discuss your preparations or strategy with other shoppers. If asked, respond with vague comments about "picking up a few things" or "getting some extras for a relative." The more unremarkable you appear, the less your cart becomes a target.

The goal is not to maximize the volume of food acquired but to maximize actual nutrition, shelf stability, and caloric density per dollar and cubic inch. One bag of rice has the same caloric content as an entire cart of many prepared foods.

Calorie-Dense, Shelf-Stable Priorities

When society stumbles, your body still needs approximately 2,000 calories daily to function optimally, along with crucial macronutrients and micronutrients. The challenge is securing these requirements in a format that won't spoil before you can consume it.

Let's break down your food acquisition priorities by nutritional category:

Carbohydrates: Your Caloric Foundation

Carbohydrates will form the foundation of your crisis nutrition strategy—they're cheap, widely available, shelf-stable, and calorie-dense. Prioritize these items:

1. **White Rice:** Not brown rice, which contains oils that can go rancid. White rice can last 30+ years properly stored. A 20lb bag contains approximately 32,500 calories—enough to provide baseline sustenance for one person for three weeks.
2. **Dried Pasta:** Nearly indefinite shelf life, high caloric density, and requires minimal water to prepare. One pound contains approximately 1,600 calories.
3. **Oats:** Old-fashioned rolled oats offer excellent nutrition, versatility, and a 2-5 year shelf life. They can be eaten with minimal preparation.
4. **Flour:** All-purpose flour in sealed containers lasts 1-2 years. While less convenient than other options, its versatility makes it valuable.
5. **Cornmeal:** Often overlooked but extremely versatile, with a shelf life of 1-2 years.

I've survived three weeks on nothing but white rice, salt, and foraged greens during a political collapse in Southeast Asia. Was it enjoyable? Not particularly. Was it effective? Absolutely. My companions who prioritized variety over caloric efficiency ran out of food in days.

Proteins: Muscle Maintenance and Satiety

Protein becomes the most challenging macronutrient to secure during extended emergencies. Focus on these options:

1. **Dried Beans and Lentils:** A complete protein when paired with rice, with a shelf life of 10+ years. One pound of dried beans provides approximately 1,500 calories and 100g of protein.
2. **Canned Meats:** Spam (*good ole spammity spam!*), corned beef, chicken, and tuna in oil (not water) offer ready-to-eat protein with 2-5 year shelf lives. Prioritize higher-fat options for added calories.
3. **Peanut Butter:** Calorie-dense with significant protein and fat. Commercial versions remain stable for 1-2 years unopened.
4. **Powdered Milk:** Eight times more protein by volume than fresh milk, with a shelf life of 1-2 years once opened, 20+ years if kept sealed.
5. **Canned Beans:** While less cost-effective than dried varieties, their ready-to-eat nature makes them valuable for immediate consumption.

During Hurricane Katrina, I observed that those who secured adequate protein maintained significantly better cognitive function and emotional stability than those subsisting primarily on carbohydrates. The difference becomes apparent within days, not weeks.

Fats: Essential Calories and Nutrient Absorption

Fats provide the highest caloric density per weight (9 calories per gram versus 4 for protein and carbs) and are essential for absorbing fat-soluble vitamins. Secure these options:

1. **Cooking Oils:** Vegetable, canola, and coconut oils provide approximately 4,000 calories per pound and last 1-2 years when unopened.
2. **Ghee/Clarified Butter:** Shelf-stable even without refrigeration, lasting 1-2 years with proper storage.
3. **Nuts and Seeds:** Calorie-dense with excellent nutritional profiles, though shelf-life concerns exist. Vacuum-sealed varieties last 1-2 years.
4. **Shortening:** Not the healthiest option but extremely shelf-stable, with 5+ year viability when unopened.
5. **Coconut Milk (Canned):** High in medium-chain triglycerides with a 2-5 year shelf life.

A tablespoon of oil added to rice provides an additional 120 calories—a 30% increase in energy value for the same volume of food. During prolonged food shortages, this efficiency becomes crucial.

Micronutrients: Preventing Deficiency Diseases

Historically, many crisis survivors who secured adequate calories still developed debilitating deficiency diseases. Prevent this with:

1. **Multivitamins:** A quality multivitamin can prevent catastrophic deficiencies during limited diets. Secure a 6-12 month supply.
2. **Canned Vegetables:** Prioritize higher-density options like spinach, carrots, and pumpkin rather than water-heavy choices like green beans.
3. **Canned Fruits:** Opt for varieties packed in juice rather than syrup for better nutritional profiles.
4. **Dried Fruits:** Calorie-dense with concentrated nutrients,

though more expensive than other options.

5. **Powdered Greens/Superfood Supplements:** Expensive but compact sources of phytonutrients with 1-2 year shelf lives.

During an extended isolation period in the Canadian wilderness, I staved off scurvy with pine needle tea when other vitamin C sources were depleted. While effective in emergencies, strategic preparation eliminates the need for such measures.

No-Cook Food Options When Power Is Unreliable

When the grid fails, your carefully acquired food supplies face a new challenge: preparation without reliable power. A surprising percentage of typical emergency food requires cooking to be safely consumed or palatable. Here's how to ensure you can actually eat what you've acquired:

Ready-to-Eat Shelf-Stable Options

These foods require absolutely no preparation and provide immediate nutrition:

1. **Meal Replacement Bars:** While expensive, options like Complete Cookie, Clif Bars, and emergency ration bars provide balanced nutrition with 3-5 year shelf lives. Secure 2-3 per person per day for the first week.

2. **Peanut Butter & Crackers:** Combining shelf-stable crackers with peanut butter creates complete protein with no preparation. Prioritize graham crackers for their higher caloric density and longer shelf life.

3. **Canned Foods with Pull-Tops:** Prioritize options that don't require a can opener—an item frequently overlooked in emergency preparations.

4. **Jerky and Meat Sticks:** Commercial varieties last 1-2 years and provide ready protein, though at higher cost-per-

calorie than other options.

5. **Nuts and Trail Mixes:** Calorie-dense with good nutritional profiles, requiring no preparation. Commercial varieties with oxygen absorbers can last 1-2 years.

During an extended power outage following an ice storm, I observed neighbors discarding hundreds of dollars of frozen food while subsisting on chips and soda. Meanwhile, those with proper no-cook options maintained relatively normal nutritional intake.

Minimal-Preparation Foods

These options require only cold water or brief ambient soaking:

1. **Instant Oats:** Unlike traditional oats, instant varieties can be prepared with cold water if necessary.
2. **Powdered Hummus:** Cold-water rehydratable with excellent nutritional profile when paired with crackers.
3. **Freeze-Dried Fruits and Vegetables:** While expensive, they rehydrate with ambient-temperature water.
4. **Powdered Peanut Butter:** Mixed with cold water, provides protein with minimal preparation.
5. **Cold-Brew Coffee Packets:** A seemingly luxury item that provides critical caffeine—which prevents withdrawal headaches and maintains alertness during stressful situations.

I've found that having even minimal-preparation food options significantly improves morale during extended emergencies. The psychological boost of something resembling "normal" food cannot be overstated.

Improvised No-Cook Meal Plans

In extended grid-down scenarios, combine your supplies into these no-cook meals:

Breakfast: Instant oats soaked in room-temperature water with peanut butter and powdered milk **Lunch:** Crackers with canned tuna or chicken, supplemented with canned vegetables **Dinner:** Canned beans with canned tomatoes and beef jerky, creating a no-cook "chili" **Snacks:** Nuts, dried fruits, and chocolate (yes, include some for morale)

A three-day rotation of similar but varied meals prevents the dangerous "food fatigue" that leads many to take risks with spoiled or unsafe food options out of boredom.

Immediate Food Preservation Techniques

When the grid fails, your refrigerator and freezer become ticking clocks. The average refrigerator maintains safe temperatures for only 4-6 hours without power, while a freezer might last 24-48 hours if left unopened. Here's how to extend the viability of your perishable foods:

Refrigerator Triage Protocol

The moment power fails, implement this protocol:

1. **Inventory and prioritize consumption.** Immediately document all perishable items, prioritizing:

- Seafood (consume within 4 hours)
- Ground meats (consume within 12 hours)
- Milk and soft cheeses (consume within 24 hours)
- Eggs and hard cheeses (viable for 2-5 days depending on ambient temperature)

1. **Convert immediately:** Using the techniques below, im-

mediately begin converting highly perishable items into shelf-stable formats.

2. **Temperature management:** Place critical items in the freezer while it remains cold, and transfer freezer items to coolers with available ice.

3. **Minimize openings:** Every time you open a powerless refrigerator, internal temperature rises by 10-20°F. Consolidate and retrieve all items in a single opening, then close firmly.

Emergency Preservation Methods

These techniques require no specialized equipment and can be implemented immediately:

1. **Salt preservation:** For meats, create a heavy brine (1 cup salt per gallon of water) and submerge cut meat for 24 hours, then air dry. This extends shelf life by 1-2 weeks at room temperature.

2. **Vinegar pickling:** For vegetables, boil equal parts vinegar and water with 1 tablespoon salt per cup of liquid. Pour over vegetables in clean jars. Extends shelf life to 2-4 weeks without refrigeration.

3. **Oil submersion:** For soft cheeses and herbs, completely submerge in olive oil in a clean container. Extends viability by 1-2 weeks.

4. **Sugar preservation:** For fruits, create a heavy syrup (2 cups sugar per quart of water), bring to boil, add fruit, and return to boil briefly. Place in clean jars. Extends shelf life to 2-4 weeks.

5. **Drying/dehydration:** For nearly anything, slice thinly and air dry on clean screens in a hot, dry location with good

airflow. Most bacteria require moisture to multiply.

During an extended grid failure in rural Argentina, I observed locals converting an entire cow into charqui (South American jerky) within hours of slaughter, without electricity or specialized equipment. The meat remained viable for months. These techniques are ancient for a reason—they work.

Strategic Use of Residual Cold

When power fails, you still have a temporary cold resource that should be strategically deployed:

1. **Freezer as cooler:** Once it's clear power won't return quickly, convert your freezer into an unpowered cooler. It's already insulated and provides an excellent environment for the ice you have.
2. **Cold transfer hierarchy:** Use melting ice first to preserve frozen raw meats, then dairy, then everything else. Every calorie preserved is one you don't need to replace.
3. **Thermal mass management:** Store filled water bottles in your freezer during normal times. During power loss, they maintain cold temperatures longer than air spaces and provide drinking water as they thaw.
4. **Communal cooling:** If neighbors have limited refrigerated items, consolidate resources into the best-insulated single unit, improving efficiency for everyone.

The longest I've maintained functional refrigeration without power is 12 days, using a combination of initial ice, good insulation, minimal openings, and strategic consumption planning.

Rationing Basics: How to Make What You Have Last

The most common survival food mistake isn't insufficient

acquisition—it's inefficient consumption. Most people raised in affluent societies have no concept of true food rationing. Here's how to stretch your supplies when necessary:

Caloric Minimums vs. Optimums

Understanding the difference between what you want, what feels normal, and what you actually need is critical:

1. **Survival minimum:** 1,200-1,500 calories daily will maintain basic function in most adults for extended periods, though with decreased energy and some muscle loss.
2. **Functional minimum:** 1,500-1,800 calories daily maintains moderate activity levels without significant physiological degradation for most adults.
3. **Optimal intake:** 2,000-2,500 calories daily supports full physical and cognitive function indefinitely.

During the Siege of Sarajevo, civilians survived on approximately 800-1,200 calories daily for months. While not ideal, understanding true minimums prevents panic when supplies appear limited.

Strategic Consumption Protocols

Follow these principles to maximize your food security:

1. **Perishable before preserved:** Always consume items in order of spoilage probability. This means refrigerated items first, then items with shorter shelf lives, saving your longest-lasting supplies for extended scenarios.
2. **Caloric density management:** As supplies diminish, prioritize calorie-dense foods. One tablespoon of oil added to rice provides 120 calories that might make the difference in maintaining function.

3. **Protein cycling:** Rather than consuming protein daily, consider protein loading every third day, which allows the body to utilize amino acids more efficiently during scarcity.
4. **Meal consolidation:** When rationing, two slightly larger meals provide better metabolic efficiency than three smaller ones, though this varies by individual.
5. **Strategic fasting:** Implementing a 16-8 intermittent fasting protocol (16 hours without food, 8-hour eating window) can extend supplies by 10-20% with minimal physical impact after adaptation.

I've personally maintained full cognitive function and moderate physical capability on 1,400 calories daily for three months during a resource constraint scenario. The key was proper macronutrient balance and strategic timing, not simply total calories.

Psychological Aspects of Rationing

The mind experiences food scarcity differently than the body:

1. **Portion control psychology:** Use smaller plates and bowls. Studies show the same amount of food appears more satisfying when it fills a container.
2. **Satiety hacking:** Consume fats and proteins first, followed by carbohydrates. This triggers earlier satiety signaling through hormonal pathways.
3. **Flavor intensity:** Increasing spices and flavorings as quantities decrease improves satisfaction. Include spices in your preparations; they're lightweight, shelf-stable, and critically important for morale.
4. **Consistent scheduling:** Maintain rigid eating times during rationing. The body adapts better to predictable intake

than variable feeding.

5. **Mindful consumption:** Eat without distractions, chew thoroughly, and focus on the experience. This significantly increases reported satiety from the same caloric intake.

After Hurricane Maria devastated Puerto Rico, I observed that families who adhered to structured rationing protocols maintained not just better nutrition but dramatically better morale than those who consumed supplies haphazardly until sudden depletion.

The Last-Minute Food Grab List

The following quick-start guide assumes you have less than 30 minutes to execute an emergency food acquisition run with limited funds. This is the no-nonsense, get-it-done list that prioritizes caloric efficiency, nutritional completeness, and shelf stability.

PRIORITY: LAST-MINUTE FOOD ACQUISITION

EMERGENCY FOOD SHOPPING LIST

GET FIRST (CRITICAL)

CALORIES

☐ **White rice (20lb bag)** ☐ **Dried pasta** ☐ **Peanut butter** ☐ **Cooking oil**

PROTEIN

☐ **Canned tuna/chicken** ☐ **Dried beans** ☐ **Spam/canned meat** ☐ **Powdered milk**

NUTRITION

☐ **Multivitamins** ☐ **Canned vegetables** ☐ **Canned fruits** ☐ **Salt**

NO-COOK

☐ **Peanut butter** ☐ **Crackers** ☐ **Canned beans** ☐ **Canned meat/fish**

GET SECOND (IF AVAILABLE)

CALORIES
☐ Oats ☐ Honey ☐ Flour ☐ Cornmeal
PROTEIN
☐ Canned beans ☐ Jerky ☐ Canned chili ☐ Protein bars
NUTRITION
☐ Dried vegetables ☐ Powdered greens ☐ Spices ☐ Bouillon cubes
NO-COOK
☐ Trail mix ☐ Meal bars ☐ Jerky ☐ Canned fruits

BASIC 30-DAY SUPPLY (ONE PERSON)

- **Rice: 20 pounds**
- **Beans: 10 pounds**
- **Peanut Butter: 3 pounds**
- **Oil: 1 gallon**
- **Multivitamins: 30-count**
- **Canned vegetables: 15 cans**

QUANTITY CALCULATIONS
For a 30-day emergency supply for one adult:
Core Survival Minimum:

- Rice: 20 pounds (32,500 calories)
- Beans: 10 pounds (15,000 calories)
- Peanut Butter: 3 pounds (15,000 calories)
- Oil: 1 gallon (30,000 calories)
- Multivitamins: 30-count bottle
- Salt: 1 pound container

- Canned vegetables: 15 cans

Total approximate calories: 92,500 (3,080 daily) **Estimated cost:** $75-125 depending on location **Total weight:** Approximately 40 pounds **Storage volume:** 2-3 cubic feet
Nutrition-Balanced Extension:

- Canned meats: 10 cans
- Powdered milk: 1 pound
- Oats: 5 pounds
- Canned fruits: 10 cans
- Honey: 2 pounds
- Dried fruits: 1 pound
- Spices: At least salt, pepper, garlic, and chili powder

Extended supply calories: 40,000 additional calories **Estimated additional cost:** $75-100 **Additional weight:** Approximately 25 pounds **Additional volume:** 1-2 cubic feet

I once had exactly 17 minutes to evacuate during a flash flood. I grabbed a 20-pound bag of rice, a 10-pound bag of beans, and cooking oil. It wasn't perfect, but it fed me for 30 days when commercial food became unavailable. Perfect is the enemy of good enough.

Remember: You're not stocking a gourmet pantry—you're creating a nutritional insurance policy. Focus on caloric density, nutritional completeness, shelf stability, and preparation flexibility. Everything else is luxury.

The difference between the prepared and the panicked isn't resources—it's knowledge and execution. You now have both. The only question is whether you'll act before the shelves empty.

4

Securing Your Home or Finding a Safe Haven

You've got water. You've got food. Now it's time to address the reason both will matter: having a secure place to consume them. The rule of threes reminds us that after air, shelter is your next priority—you can survive three hours in extreme conditions without adequate shelter. But let's be clear about what "shelter" means in a crisis context: it's not just a roof and walls—it's a defensible position that protects you from environmental threats, human threats, and the psychological degradation that comes with exposure and insecurity.

I've seen well-supplied survivors lose everything because they neglected basic shelter security. During Hurricane Katrina, I witnessed families with ample water and food supplies become victims within 72 hours because they hadn't secured their perimeter. Conversely, I've seen resourceful individuals with minimal supplies thrive for weeks in homes that wouldn't impress anyone under normal circumstances, but which had been systematically hardened against intrusion and environmental threats.

The shelter question comes down to a binary decision that must be made immediately: bug in or bug out? Stay or go? *(there should be that song by The Clash on repeat in your head!)* Defend your current position or seek a more defensible one? This chapter will guide you through that decision-making process and provide immediate action steps for either choice. First, though, let's talk about how to secure what you already have.

Quick Home Fortification Techniques

Your home was designed for comfort, convenience, and aesthetics—not security. In normal times, this makes perfect sense. In crisis times, it makes you vulnerable. The good news? You can dramatically improve your home's defensive position in under an hour with materials you already have.

Let's start with the brutal truth: the average American home can be entered in under 60 seconds by a determined intruder. Front doors typically have a single deadbolt that can be kicked in with minimal effort. First-floor windows are usually single-pane glass that can be broken silently. Sliding doors can often be popped off their tracks with a screwdriver. We're going to fix all of that—fast.

Rapid Door Hardening

Your doors are your primary vulnerability. Hardening them is your first priority:

1. **The Chair Jamb Method:** Place a straight-backed chair under the doorknob at a 45-degree angle. This creates a triangular support structure that can withstand 600+ pounds of force—more than most human kicks. For maximum effectiveness, place the chair's back just under the doorknob, with the legs angled away from the door.
2. **The Screw Method:** If you have a power drill, use 3-inch

screws to replace the half-inch screws typically found in strike plates and hinges. This extends the security connection from the door frame into the structural studs of the wall. A door secured this way can withstand most battering attempts short of a police-style ram.

3. **The Barricade Method:** For sliding doors or inward-opening doors, place heavy furniture directly against them. Bookshelves, dressers, and refrigerators make excellent impromptu barricades. The key is creating mass that must be moved to gain entry.

4. **The Secondary Lock Method:** Additional security can be added using ordinary household items. A fork can be bent and wedged into the door track of a sliding door. A portable door lock (if you have one) can be installed in seconds. Even a doorstop wedged under an inward-opening door adds significant resistance.

During civil unrest in South America, a family successfully defended their modest apartment using nothing but strategically arranged furniture and makeshift door reinforcements. The would-be intruders moved on to easier targets within minutes—which is exactly what you want.

Window Security Acceleration

Windows represent your second most vulnerable entry point. Here's how to secure them rapidly:

1. **The Hurricane Film Method:** If you have clear packing tape, apply it in a cross-hatch pattern over window glass. While this won't prevent breaking, it will prevent the silent removal of glass panes and make entry more time-consuming and noisy.

2. **The Visual Deterrent Method:** Close all blinds and curtains immediately. This prevents potential threats from conducting reconnaissance on your supplies or occupants. If curtains are unavailable, tape newspaper, cardboard, or sheets over windows.

3. **The Noise Alert Method:** Place empty cans, bottles, or other noise-making objects on windowsills. While not preventing entry, they create an early warning system that buys precious response time.

4. **The Barrier Method:** For ground-floor windows, place furniture—preferably heavy items like bookshelves or dressers—directly in front of them. This creates both a physical and psychological barrier to entry.

I once observed a neighborhood in a post-hurricane scenario where homes with visibly secured windows were bypassed entirely by opportunistic looters, while unsecured homes were systematically targeted. The perception of security can be as effective as security itself.

Perimeter Enhancement

Your property boundary provides your first opportunity to deter unwanted visitors:

1. **The Grey Man Approach:** The most effective security often involves not appearing to have anything worth taking. Remove any external indicators of preparedness—generator noise, visible supplies, or obvious security measures can attract unwanted attention. Projecting an appearance of "nothing to see here" can be your best first-line defense.

2. **The Obstacle Course Method:** Create physical deterrents along obvious approach paths. Furniture, garden equip-

ment, or even scattered toys can break up direct access routes and make silent approach more difficult. In urban environments, these obstacles also force potential threats to make noise or expose themselves longer during approach.

3. **The Natural Barrier Method:** Utilize landscaping features as security assets. Thorny bushes under windows, gravel paths that make silent approach impossible, or even strategically parked vehicles can channel movement to areas you can more easily monitor.

4. **The Visual Monitoring Setup:** Establish observation points that allow you to monitor approaches without exposing yourself. A small mirror positioned in a window can provide a wide field of view while keeping you out of sight.

During extended power outages after ice storms, I've noticed that homes appearing "abandoned" or "already looted" were typically left alone, while those showing obvious signs of preparation drew unwanted attention. Sometimes the best security is invisibility.

Evaluating Your Current Shelter's Viability

Not all shelters are created equal. Your beautiful suburban colonial with floor-to-ceiling windows might be a House Beautiful feature in normal times but a security nightmare during civil unrest. Conversely, that modest garden-level apartment with limited entry points might suddenly become prime real estate. Let's assess what you're working with.

The Shelter Viability Index

Rate your current shelter on these critical factors:

1. **Access Control (1-10):** How many entry points exist? Can they be effectively monitored and secured? Fewer entry points are better—a home with 12+ potential access points becomes extremely difficult to secure without a team.

2. **Resource Availability (1-10):** Does your location have independent water sources (well, natural spring, rain catchment potential)? Is passive solar heating available? Can you cook without external utilities? Higher self-sufficiency equals higher viability.

3. **Visibility/Privacy (1-10):** Can your activities be easily observed from outside? Can you observe external approaches without exposing yourself? Greater privacy equals greater security.

4. **Structural Integrity (1-10):** How well will your shelter withstand environmental threats? Is it flood-prone? Wind-resistant? Fire-resistant? Stronger structures provide better long-term viability.

5. **Community Context (1-10):** Is your shelter isolated or part of a community? Are neighbors potential allies or threats? Do natural surveillance opportunities exist? Community support networks dramatically increase shelter viability.

Add these scores. Below 25 points indicates serious viability concerns that may justify relocation if options exist. Above 40 suggests a highly defensible position worth maintaining. Between 25-40 requires the immediate hardening techniques described above.

I've seen families abandon perfectly viable 45-point shelters out of panic, only to end up in 20-point situations that dramatically reduced their survival chances. Conversely, I've watched unprepared individuals transform 30-point shelters into 40-

point shelters through simple, methodical improvements. Realistic assessment saves lives.

The Resource Extension Assessment

Your shelter's viability is directly connected to how long its critical systems will function. Conduct this rapid assessment:

1. **Water systems:** If municipal water fails, how many gallons can you store? Is rain catchment possible? Are natural water sources accessible within a secure perimeter? Every human needs a minimum of 1-2 gallons daily.

2. **Sanitation systems:** If municipal sewage fails, what alternatives exist? Can you create a temporary composting toilet? Is greywater disposal possible without creating health hazards?

3. **Temperature regulation:** Without power, how will your shelter maintain survivable temperatures? In cold climates, do you have alternative heating methods that don't require electricity? In hot climates, can you create passive cooling?

4. **Food preparation:** Can you cook without conventional utilities? Do you have fuel for a minimum of 30 days? Are non-fuel cooking methods available?

5. **Security systems:** Without power, do you have manual locks, barriers, and monitoring capabilities? Can you secure critical areas even if electronic systems fail?

During an extended winter power outage in New England, seemingly well-prepared homes became uninhabitable within 72 hours as interior temperatures dropped below freezing. Meanwhile, modest homes with wood stoves and manual systems maintained survivable conditions indefinitely. The simplest systems often prove most resilient.

Essential Tools for Emergency Repairs and Security

Tools multiply human capability. In crisis situations, having the right tools can be the difference between a minor inconvenience and a shelter failure that forces relocation. Here's what you need to gather immediately:

The Core Emergency Tool Kit

These items address 90% of likely shelter emergencies and should be gathered into a single, accessible container:

1. **Multi-tool or combination of basic tools:** Hammer, screwdrivers (flathead and Phillips), pliers, adjustable wrench. These handle most immediate repair needs.
2. **Cordless drill with charged battery:** If available, this dramatically accelerates securing doors and windows. If power is already out, manual screwdrivers become essential.
3. **Pry bar/crowbar:** Useful for both emergency access (to your own locked areas if keys are lost) and creating materials for repairs and barricades.
4. **Duct tape, electrical tape, and plumber's tape:** The universal repair materials. Each serves specific functions but all create immediate, temporary solutions to critical failures.
5. **Heavy-duty trash bags:** Beyond waste management, these serve as impromptu waterproofing, material carriers, and even emergency shelter components.
6. **Zip ties in various sizes:** Perhaps the most versatile fastening system for non-load-bearing emergency repairs.
7. **Work gloves:** Protect your hands during repairs. In crisis situations, even minor hand injuries can become debilitating without proper medical care.
8. **Headlamp or flashlight with spare batteries:** Repairs

often happen in low-light conditions during emergencies. Hands-free lighting is particularly valuable.

9. **Permanent marker:** For labeling, marking, and communication when electronic options fail.

10. **Utility knife with spare blades:** For cutting, shaping, and modifying materials during repairs.

During Hurricane Sandy, a retired contractor saved six neighboring apartments from severe water damage using nothing but this basic kit and materials scavenged from the buildings. The ability to implement immediate repairs often determines whether a shelter remains viable.

Security-Specific Tools

These items specifically enhance your security posture:

1. **Door security bar or barricade:** Commercial options are best, but improvised versions using angled 2×4 lumber can be equally effective.

2. **Window security film or alternative:** Commercial security film is ideal, but clear packing tape can serve as a temporary substitute.

3. **Motion detection devices:** Battery-powered units are best, but even simple trip wires connected to noise-making objects serve the purpose.

4. **Communications equipment:** Two-way radios allow coordination between security positions without shouting or exposing positions.

5. **Observation tools:** Binoculars or a monocular for distant observation; small mirrors for observing around corners or through windows without exposure.

An elderly couple successfully defended their home during post-hurricane looting using nothing but strategically placed wind chimes as alert systems and a series of pre-positioned mirrors that allowed them to monitor all approaches from a single, secure location. Ingenuity often outperforms expensive security systems.

Improvised Barriers and Entry Deterrents

When conventional security fails or proves inadequate, improvisation becomes essential. Your home contains dozens of potential security assets that can be repurposed within minutes. Here's how to identify and deploy them:

Rapid Barrier Deployment

These techniques create substantial physical obstacles using ordinary household items:

1. **The Bookcase Barricade:** Bookshelves make ideal barricades due to their weight and structural integrity. Place them at 45-degree angles against doors, with the shelf side facing the door. This creates a wedge that becomes more secure when pressure is applied.
2. **The Furniture Wall:** Couch cushions might seem soft, but when stacked between two anchored pieces of furniture, they create a surprisingly effective bullet and impact-resistant barrier. Layer multiple cushions for increased protection.
3. **The Appliance Obstacle:** Refrigerators, washing machines, and other heavy appliances create nearly immovable barriers when water-filled or loaded with heavy items. Position them to channel movement through predetermined paths that you can monitor.
4. **The Bedframe Blockade:** Metal bed frames, particularly

the angle-iron variety, can be disassembled and repurposed as door and window reinforcements. The L-shaped metal pieces are ideal for reinforcing door hinges and frames.

During civil unrest in Eastern Europe, residents created elaborate internal barricade systems using ordinary furniture that effectively compartmentalized their homes, making unauthorized movement nearly impossible even if the main entry was breached.

Psychological Deterrents

Physical barriers work best when complemented by psychological deterrents that discourage approach:

1. **The False Occupancy Indicator:** Create the impression of greater numbers through multiple light sources, voices (radio positioned near different windows), and movement (hanging sheets that move with air currents).
2. **The Previous Targeting Illusion:** Where appropriate, create the appearance that your location has already been looted or abandoned—disrupted entrances, strategic but minor exterior damage, or "X" markings similar to those used by search teams.
3. **The Uncertainty Principle:** Remove or obscure house numbers and familiar landmarks that would allow targeting of your specific location. In confusion, most opportunistic threats move to more certain targets.
4. **The Noise Discipline Protocol:** Implement strict noise control, particularly during night hours. Sound carries much further than most people realize, and auditory signatures often attract unwanted attention before visual

confirmation occurs.

Homes creating uncertainty about occupancy status or defensive capability were typically bypassed in favor of clearly occupied, clearly undefended alternatives. Exploiting the risk-averse nature of opportunistic threats is a powerful defensive strategy.

Specialized Zone Defense

Rather than attempting to secure your entire shelter equally, consider a layered, zone-based approach:

1. **The Safe Room Concept:** Designate and reinforce one room as your final defensive position. This room should contain essential supplies, communications, and your strongest security measures. During heightened threats, withdraw to this position rather than attempting to defend your entire perimeter.

2. **The Sacrificial Zone Strategy:** Designate less-essential areas of your shelter as "sacrificial zones" that intruders might access without compromising your core security. These areas can even contain decoy supplies or distractions that occupy attention while you maintain control of critical areas.

3. **The Channelization Technique:** Use furniture, barriers, and obstacles to create predetermined movement paths within your shelter. These should channel any unauthorized movement toward areas you can easily monitor or that create tactical disadvantages for intruders.

4. **The Safe Withdrawal Route:** Always maintain at least one pre-planned, secured route for emergency evacuation if your shelter becomes untenable. This route should be known only to authorized occupants and should ideally

exit through an unexpected access point.

During extended civil disruption in South America, families successfully maintained security by concentrating their defensive resources on a single "core" area rather than the entire property. This approach recognized the reality of limited personnel and resources while providing sustainable security.

Relocation Criteria: When to Bug Out Versus Bug In

The most critical shelter decision you'll make is whether to stay or go. (*The Clash again!*) This decision must be based on objective criteria, not emotional reactions or preconceptions. Here's how to make that determination rapidly and correctly:

The Stay (Bug In) Factors

These factors support a decision to remain in your current shelter:

1. **Resource Advantage:** Your current location contains essential supplies that cannot be transported effectively. If you've stockpiled significant water, food, or medical supplies, abandoning them creates immediate disadvantage.
2. **Knowledge Advantage:** You have deep familiarity with your current environment, including defensive positions, resource locations, community dynamics, and potential allies. This "home field advantage" is easily underestimated but critically important.
3. **Security Advantage:** Your current shelter has been hardened, has limited access points, or possesses natural defensive features that would be difficult to replicate elsewhere.
4. **Health Limitations:** Any occupants have medical conditions, mobility restrictions, or other special needs that would be compromised by relocation.

5. **External Threat Pattern:** The nature of the threat (weather event, civil unrest, infrastructure failure) is likely to resolve within a time period your current supplies can accommodate.

I've observed families abandon relatively secure positions with abundant supplies due to fear or incomplete information, only to face much greater dangers in unfamiliar environments with minimal resources. The decision to stay should be your default unless compelling factors indicate otherwise.

The Go (Bug Out) Factors

These factors support a decision to relocate:

1. **Immediate Environmental Threat:** Your current location faces imminent danger from fire, flooding, structural collapse, chemical hazard, or other non-negotiable threat to life safety.

2. **Resource Exhaustion:** Your essential supplies (particularly water) are depleted beyond sustainable levels with no replenishment options available.

3. **Security Compromise:** Your location has been specifically targeted by threats you cannot reasonably defend against, or security measures have been breached beyond repair.

4. **Viable Alternative Available:** You have a specifically prepared alternative location with confirmed availability, accessible by a known route, with equivalent or superior resources already in place.

5. **Authoritative Evacuation Order:** Legitimate authorities with accurate threat information have ordered evacuation AND you have confirmed the evacuation route is actually viable.

During Hurricane Katrina, unnecessary evacuations placed some families in greater danger. The key is objective assessment rather than emotional reaction.

The Vulnerability Window

Understand that the period of active relocation represents your moment of maximum vulnerability:

1. **The Transportation Risk:** Moving typically requires using predetermined routes that may be monitored, congested, or compromised. Vehicle dependency creates fuel, mechanical, and mobility constraints that don't exist in stationary positions.
2. **The Visibility Factor:** Movement inherently increases your visibility and exposure to potential threats, both human and environmental.
3. **The Resource Limitation:** You can transport only a fraction of the resources you can store at a fixed location. This creates immediate supply constraints.
4. **The Intelligence Gap:** Moving to a new area creates an immediate knowledge deficit regarding local conditions, threats, and resources.

For these reasons, the decision to relocate should never be made lightly or without compelling justification. I've observed a consistent pattern across multiple disaster scenarios: those who relocated without absolute necessity typically faced greater challenges than those who improved their existing positions.

The 60-Minute Home Security Upgrade

When crisis looms, minutes matter. The following protocol represents the most efficient sequence for maximizing your shelter security in minimal time. This is not a theoretical exercise—it's a battle-tested sequence refined through multiple disaster responses.

60-MINUTE HOME SECURITY UPGRADE

0-15 MINUTES

PERIMETER SECURITY
- ☐ Remove external valuables
- ☐ Secure outdoor tools
- ☐ Clear approach paths of clutter

ENTRY SECURITY
- ☐ Reinforce main entry door
- ☐ Place furniture barricades
- ☐ Secure pet entries

INTERNAL SECURITY
- ☐ Establish safe room
- ☐ Collect and stage tools
- ☐ Designate security zones

MONITORING
- ☐ Position observation mirrors
- ☐ Set up noise alerts
- ☐ Establish communication system

15-30 MINUTES

PERIMETER SECURITY
- ☐ Apply window coverings

☐ Create visual deterrents
☐ Implement noise deterrents

ENTRY SECURITY
☐ Reinforce secondary doors
☐ Apply window security measures
☐ Disable garage door openers

INTERNAL SECURITY
☐ Relocate essential supplies
☐ Create internal barriers
☐ Establish evacuation routes

MONITORING
☐ Position internal alerts
☐ Create movement channels
☐ Establish signal system

30-45 MINUTES

PERIMETER SECURITY
☐ Test exterior sight lines
☐ Position exterior deterrents
☐ Conceal high-value items

ENTRY SECURITY
☐ Test all entry barriers
☐ Reinforce vulnerable points
☐ Create backup barriers

INTERNAL SECURITY

☐ Distribute essential tools
☐ Create decoy supplies
☐ Establish sleep positions

MONITORING
☐ Test all alert systems
☐ Conduct security walkthrough
☐ Assign monitoring shifts

45-60 MINUTES

PERIMETER SECURITY
☐ Final perimeter check
☐ Implement gray man measures
☐ Secure unused buildings

ENTRY SECURITY
☐ Verify all locks/barriers
☐ Ensure silent entry option
☐ Create access protocols

INTERNAL SECURITY
☐ Conduct final resource check
☐ Verify safe room security
☐ Brief all occupants

MONITORING
☐ Establish normal patterns
☐ Implement noise discipline
☐ Final security briefing

EXECUTION NOTES

The sequence above is deliberately designed for maximum efficiency. Some critical principles:

1. **Work from exterior to interior:** Secure your perimeter first, then work inward toward your safe room. This ensures that if your work is interrupted, your most critical areas receive priority.
2. **Verify through testing:** Don't assume barriers will work—physically test them. Many improvised security measures fail under actual stress if not properly implemented.
3. **Layer your defenses:** No single security measure is fail-proof. Overlapping systems create defense in depth that remains effective even if individual measures fail.
4. **Brief all occupants:** Everyone in your shelter should understand security protocols, alert signals, and response procedures. Security breaches often occur not because measures failed but because they weren't properly understood or implemented by all occupants.
5. **Maintain operational security:** The effectiveness of your security measures depends partly on their invisibility to potential threats. Maintain a "normal" external appearance while implementing internal security.

In an actual crisis situation, I've completed this exact protocol in 47 minutes with limited assistance. The result was a standard suburban home transformed into a significantly hardened position that deterred multiple approach attempts during the subsequent unrest. These principles work—if implemented decisively and correctly.

The objective isn't creating an impenetrable fortress—it's creating a hardened position that encourages potential threats to seek easier alternatives. In crisis scenarios, most opportunistic threats follow the path of least resistance. Your job is ensuring that path leads elsewhere.

Your home can be your castle—but only if you transform it from a convenience-oriented environment into a security-oriented one. Start now. The clock is ticking.

5

First Aid and Medications: Your Emergency Medical Plan

When the world goes sideways, medical infrastructure is typically the first system to be overwhelmed and the last to recover. I've stood in emergency rooms during crisis situations watching triage nurses turn away patients with conditions that would warrant immediate attention during normal times. I've seen pharmacies emptied within hours of disaster declarations, leaving chronic condition sufferers desperately searching for medications they need to survive. These aren't apocalyptic fantasies—they're predictable patterns I've observed across three decades of disaster response work.

Let me be brutally honest: in a crisis scenario, your health instantly becomes your responsibility in a way most Americans haven't experienced since the early 20th century. The convenient safety net of dial 911 and wait ten minutes disappears. The luxury of urgent care centers with minimal wait times evaporates. The reassuring availability of prescription refills becomes a distant memory.

The good news? You can prepare for this reality even at the

last minute. This chapter isn't about becoming an emergency physician overnight—it's about establishing the minimum viable medical preparedness to bridge the gap until professional systems recover. We'll focus on the most common emergencies, the most essential medications, and the most critical sanitation practices that prevent medical problems before they begin.

Remember: in crisis medicine, preventing emergencies is infinitely more effective than treating them. Let's get started.

The Last-Minute First Aid Kit Assembly

Your medical strategy begins with assembling a functional first aid kit. Forget the cute pre-packaged kits with cartoon characters and fifteen band-aids—those are designed for marketing, not emergencies. We're building something useful with what you have available.

Start by gathering these essential components from around your home. You likely have 80% of what you need already; you just need to consolidate it into a single, accessible container.

Core Components: The Non-Negotiables

These items address the most common and most dangerous emergency scenarios:

Bleeding Control Materials: Bleeding kills fastest, making it your first priority. Gather:

- Clean cloth (T-shirts, sheets, towels cut into squares)
- Adhesive bandages in various sizes
- Medical or duct tape
- Elastic bandage wraps (ACE bandages)
- Sanitary pads and tampons (excellent for wound packing)
- Clean plastic bags for pressure dressings

Infection Prevention: In disaster conditions, minor wounds frequently become life-threatening infections. Collect:

- Antibiotic ointment (Neosporin, Polysporin)
- Isopropyl alcohol (91% preferred over 70%)
- Hydrogen peroxide
- Povidone-iodine (Betadine) if available
- Hand sanitizer (60%+ alcohol content)
- Bar soap (remarkably effective and stable long-term)

Pain and Inflammation Control: Pain management becomes crucial for functionality. Gather:

- Acetaminophen (Tylenol)
- Ibuprofen (Advil, Motrin)
- Aspirin (also critical for suspected heart attacks)
- Any prescription pain medications you legitimately possess
- Cold packs (instant chemical type if available)
- Heat packs or hot water bottle

Allergy and Respiratory Support: Respiratory issues are common in disasters. Include:

- Antihistamines (Benadryl, Zyrtec, Claritin)
- Decongestants (Sudafed, Afrin)
- Any rescue inhalers for asthma sufferers
- Honey for cough suppression (not for children under 1 year)
- Cough drops or hard candies

Gastrointestinal Management: Digestive issues become prevalent during stress and changed eating patterns. Collect:

- Anti-diarrheal medication (Imodium, Pepto-Bismol)
- Laxatives (dietary changes often cause constipation)
- Electrolyte replacement (sports drinks, Pedialyte, or salt/-sugar packets)
- Activated charcoal if available (for certain poisoning scenarios)

During Hurricane Maria, a man's minor foot laceration developed into a life-threatening infection within 72 hours due to lack of basic wound care supplies. His eventual evacuation required a military helicopter that could have been avoided with a $3 tube of antibiotic ointment and proper cleaning. Don't be that person.

Instrument and Application Tools

These items allow you to effectively use your core supplies:

Basic Instruments:

- Scissors (preferably trauma shears with blunt tips)
- Tweezers (splinter removal becomes crucial)
- Safety pins (multiple uses including drain creation)
- Digital thermometer
- Magnifying glass for wound inspection and splinter location
- Penlight or small flashlight

Application Materials:

- Cotton balls and cotton swabs
- Clean cloths for cleaning and applying medications
- Disposable gloves (non-latex if allergies present)
- Small cups for measuring liquid medications

- Medicine droppers or oral syringes for precise dosing
- Tongue depressors or popsicle sticks as splints or application tools

Immobilization Equipment:

- SAM splint if available (or magazines secured with tape)
- Elastic bandages for compression and support
- Triangle bandages for slings and bindings
- Duct tape (the universal medical supply in emergencies)
- Safety pins for securing bandages and slings

During a remote wilderness emergency, I once stabilized a compound fracture using only a SAM splint, an ACE bandage, and duct tape. The patient maintained limb function through a 22-hour evacuation. Proper immobilization dramatically improves outcomes for orthopedic injuries.

Improvised Alternatives When Supplies Are Unavailable

When commercial medical supplies are unavailable, these household items can serve as functional substitutes:

For Wound Cleaning:

- White vinegar diluted 1:3 with clean water (effective antimicrobial)
- Strong liquor (vodka, rum, whiskey at 80 proof/40%+ alcohol)
- Boiled salt water (1 tablespoon salt per quart of water)

For Wound Covering:

- Clean cotton T-shirts torn into strips
- Freshly laundered sheets cut into squares
- Feminine hygiene products (unscented, no additives)
- Coffee filters (surprisingly effective for minor wounds)

For Immobilization:

- Magazines rolled and taped for rigid support
- Cardboard cut and folded for customized splints
- Pillows secured with belts for larger joint stabilization
- Wooden spoons or rulers as finger splints

For Medication Administration:

- Honey as cough suppressant and wound treatment
- Diluted sports drinks for electrolyte replacement
- Baking soda paste for insect bites and minor burns
- Strong black tea bags (cooled) for eye infections and minor burns

During extended flooding in Southeast Asia, local medics successfully used banana leaves as sterile wound covering after briefly exposing them to flame. The waxy surface provided excellent barrier protection when commercial dressings were unavailable. Improvisation based on scientific principles saves lives.

Essential Medications and Substitutions in a Crisis

Medication management becomes critical during extended emergencies. Understanding both conventional medications and their potential alternatives can mean the difference between maintaining functionality and becoming a casualty. Let's address the most essential categories:

Critical Prescription Medications: Your Top Priority

Some medications cannot be missed without life-threatening consequences. Prioritize securing these immediately:

Insulin and Diabetes Medications:

- Insulin typically requires refrigeration but can remain viable at room temperature for 28 days
- Stock glucose monitoring supplies and hypoglycemia treatments (glucose tablets, honey)
- If insulin becomes unavailable, implement strict carbohydrate restriction to minimize requirements

Cardiovascular Medications:

- Blood pressure medications, particularly beta-blockers, should never be stopped suddenly
- Anti-arrhythmic for heart rhythm disorders are generally non-substitutable
- Blood thinners may require managed tapering rather than abrupt discontinuation

Seizure Medications:

- Anti-seizure medications require strict adherence to prevent breakthrough seizures
- Sudden discontinuation can trigger status epilepticus, a life-threatening condition
- No reliable over-the-counter substitutes exist

Psychiatric Medications:

- Many psychiatric medications cause dangerous withdrawal syndromes if stopped suddenly
- Prioritize maintenance of antipsychotics and mood stabilizers
- For SSRIs/SNRIs, tapering is much preferred but sudden discontinuation is rarely immediately life-threatening though distressing

Respiratory Medications:

- Rescue inhalers for asthma and COPD should be prioritized above almost all other medications
- Spacers can be improvised from plastic bottles in emergencies
- Breathing techniques such as pursed-lip breathing can help manage symptoms when medications are unavailable

During an extended winter storm isolation, a rural family maintained an elderly member's heart medication regimen when roads became impassable. By coordinating with neighbors across a five-mile radius, they assembled a three-week supply through shared partial prescriptions. Community medication coordination can be a literal lifesaver.

Over-the-Counter Essentials: The Foundation of Crisis Medicine

These non-prescription medications address the most common medical issues and should be stockpiled in adequate quantities:

Analgesics (Pain Relievers):

- Acetaminophen (Tylenol): 500 count bottle minimum
- Ibuprofen (Advil, Motrin): 500 count bottle minimum
- Aspirin: 300 count bottle minimum (also serves as emergency cardiac medication)
- Topical analgesics (Bengay, lidocaine patches) for localized pain

Gastrointestinal Medications:

- Antacids (Tums, Rolaids): 500 count minimum
- Anti-diarrheal medication (Imodium): 200 count minimum
- Laxatives: Both osmotic (Miralax) and stimulant (Ex-Lax) varieties
- Anti-nausea options (Dramamine, ginger supplements)

Allergy and Respiratory Medications:

- Antihistamines: Both sedating (Benadryl) and non-sedating (Claritin, Zyrtec)
- Decongestants (Sudafed) - note that pseudoephedrine may require ID in some locations
- Cough suppressants containing dextromethorphan
- Saline nasal spray (can be improvised with salt water)

Topical Medications:

- Antibiotic ointments (Neosporin, Polysporin)
- Antifungal creams (Lotrimin, Lamisil)
- Hydrocortisone cream for skin irritation and allergic reac-

tions
- Burn gel or aloe vera gel

Electrolyte Replacement:

- Oral rehydration salts or commercial solutions (Pedialyte)
- Sports drink powder (less optimal but functional)
- DIY version: 6 level teaspoons sugar, 1/2 level teaspoon salt, 1 liter clean water

I once treated a group of stranded hikers suffering from dehydration after attempting to treat diarrheal illness without proper electrolyte replacement. They had water but had depleted their sodium and potassium levels to dangerous levels. Remember: water alone cannot replace electrolytes lost through illness or exertion.

Herbal and Alternative Medications: When Conventional Options Fail

While less predictable than pharmaceutical options, these alternatives have historical efficacy when conventional medications become unavailable:

Willow Bark:

- Contains salicin, similar to aspirin
- Effective for pain and fever reduction
- Preparation: Steep 1-2 teaspoons bark in boiling water for 10-15 minutes

Garlic:

- Broad-spectrum antimicrobial properties
- Most effective when crushed and applied directly to wounds
- Internal consumption may help with respiratory infections

Ginger:

- Effective anti-nausea treatment comparable to some pharmaceuticals
- Also provides anti-inflammatory effects
- Preparation: Tea from fresh or dried root, or direct consumption

Turmeric:

- Contains curcumin, a powerful anti-inflammatory
- Most effective when combined with black pepper to increase bioavailability
- Apply as paste to wounds or consume as tea

Honey:

- Effective wound treatment due to antimicrobial properties
- Cough suppressant supported by clinical studies
- Should be raw, unfiltered honey for maximum benefit

During extended grid-down scenarios in rural settings, I've observed remarkably effective wound management using honey-impregnated dressings when pharmaceutical options were unavailable. The osmotic and antimicrobial properties create an environment hostile to bacterial growth while supporting tissue healing.

Basic Treatment Protocols for Common Emergencies

When professional medical care is unavailable, following established protocols for common emergencies can dramatically improve outcomes. These are not substitutes for professional care but bridge gaps until such care becomes available.

Wound Management: The Foundation of Crisis Medicine

Wounds present the most common emergency scenario in crisis situations. Proper management prevents infection and promotes healing:

Initial Assessment:

- Determine wound type: laceration, puncture, abrasion, avulsion
- Assess bleeding severity: capillary (slow oozing), venous (steady flow), arterial (spurting)
- Look for embedded objects, contamination, or signs of infection

Bleeding Control Protocol:

- Apply direct pressure with clean cloth
- Elevate wounded area above heart level if possible
- For severe bleeding, apply pressure to arterial pressure points:
- Arm wounds: Compress brachial artery inside upper arm
- Leg wounds: Compress femoral artery in groin crease
- Apply tourniquet only for life-threatening extremity hemorrhage as a last resort

Cleaning Protocol:

- Irrigate wound vigorously with clean water (pressure improves debris removal)
- Clean surrounding skin with soap and water, working away from wound
- Apply antiseptic solution (iodine, alcohol) to wound edges only
- Remove all visible debris with tweezers (sterilized if possible)

Closure Assessment:

- Small wounds (<1 inch) with clean edges: Consider adhesive closure
- Larger wounds or those under tension: Leave open with moist dressing
- Deep punctures: DO NOT close; leave open to drain
- Facial or high-mobility area wounds: Prioritize for closure if possible

Dressing Application:

- Apply thin layer of antibiotic ointment if available
- Cover with non-adherent dressing (improvise with plastic wrap if necessary)
- Secure with bandage, keeping tension moderate
- Redress daily, assessing for infection signs

I once treated a construction worker who sustained a significant hand laceration during disaster cleanup. By implementing proper wound irrigation and leaving the wound open with daily dressing changes, we prevented infection despite working in contaminated conditions for a week before medical evacuation became possible.

Fracture and Dislocation Management: Preventing Disability

Orthopedic injuries increase dramatically during disasters. Proper stabilization preserves function:

Assessment Protocol:

- Look for deformity, swelling, and bruising
- Compare to uninjured side for symmetry
- Check circulation, sensation, and movement below injury
- Assess for open fracture (bone penetrating skin)

Immobilization Technique:

- Stabilize joint above and below suspected fracture
- Maintain found position—do not attempt realignment unless circulation is compromised
- Pad rigid supports to prevent pressure injury
- Secure with bandages, cloth strips, or tape
- Recheck circulation every 30 minutes after immobilization

Specific Fracture Approaches:

- Arm fractures: Create sling and swathe with triangle bandage
- Leg fractures: Splint from hip to ankle when possible
- Clavicle: Figure-eight bandage or sling
- Rib: Supportive bandaging only if necessary for pain control

Dislocation Management:

- Shoulder: Support in position of comfort, do not attempt reduction
- Digits: Gentle traction may realign if attempted immediately
- Patella: Straighten leg slowly with gentle superior pressure on patella
- Jaw: Downward pressure on lower molars using thumbs (wrapped in cloth)

During post-earthquake response work, I guided a family through proper immobilization of a child's forearm fracture using rolled magazines and duct tape. The improvised splint maintained bone alignment through three days of delayed evacuation, preventing the permanent disability that might have resulted from improper movement.

Burn Management: Preventing Infection and Scarring

Burns are common in disaster scenarios, particularly when people use unfamiliar heating and cooking methods:

Severity Assessment:

- First-degree: Red, painful, no blisters (like mild sunburn)
- Second-degree: Blistered, extremely painful, moist appearance
- Third-degree: Leathery, painless, dry appearance with white, brown, or black color

Immediate Treatment Protocol:

- Stop the burning process: Remove from heat source, extinguish flames
- Cool the burn with room temperature water for 10-15 minutes
- DO NOT use ice, butter, or oils
- DO NOT break blisters
- Remove jewelry and constrictive items immediately before swelling occurs

Dressing Technique:

- First-degree: May be left open or covered with aloe vera gel
- Second-degree: Cover with non-adherent dressing after cooling
- Third-degree: Cover loosely with clean, dry sheet or pillowcase; seek medical attention

Ongoing Care:

- Keep burn clean and covered
- Change dressings daily using sterile technique
- Monitor for infection: increasing pain, redness, swelling, pus, foul odor
- Maintain hydration—large burns significantly increase fluid requirements

A family during an extended power outage experienced multiple burn injuries while using an unfamiliar kerosene heater. By implementing proper cooling and sterile dressing changes, they prevented the infection that so often complicates burn injuries in austere conditions.

Sanitation and Disease Prevention in Disaster Conditions

Disease prevention becomes paramount when medical resources are scarce. Historically, more disaster deaths result from secondary disease than from the initial event. Implementing proper sanitation protocols creates your most effective medical intervention.

Water Safety Protocols: Preventing Waterborne Illness

Contaminated water becomes the primary disease vector in many disasters:

Treatment Hierarchy:

- Boiling: Rolling boil for 1 minute (3 minutes at high altitude)
- Chemical treatment: Chlorine bleach (2 drops per quart), iodine, or purification tablets
- Filtration: Commercial filters or improvised sand/charcoal filters
- UV treatment: SODIS method using clear bottles in direct sunlight for 6+ hours

Storage Standards:

- Use food-grade containers only
- Maintain separate containers for drinking water and sanitation water
- Store in cool, dark location when possible
- Rotate regularly, even in emergencies

Consumption Precautions:

- Treat all untested water sources as contaminated

- Use separate drinking cups or bottles for each person
- Wash hands before handling water containers
- When in doubt, re-treat water before consumption

During flood response work, I observed one household maintain completely illness-free status by implementing religious water purification protocols while neighboring families experienced widespread gastrointestinal illness. The difference was procedural discipline, not resource availability.

Waste Management Systems: The Foundation of Disease Prevention

Human waste becomes an immediate health hazard when normal disposal systems fail:

Temporary Toilet Solutions:

- 5-gallon bucket lined with heavy-duty trash bag
- Add layer of sawdust, shredded paper, or soil after each use
- Secure lid when not in use
- Replace bag when half full

Outdoor Options:

- Dig trench latrines at least 200 feet from any water source
- Minimum 12 inches deep with excavated soil piled beside trench
- Cover each deposit with soil
- Close and mark when filled to within 4 inches of surface

Waste Disposal Protocol:

- Bury human waste at least 12 inches deep
- Use separate disposal area for pet waste
- Manage feminine hygiene products as biological waste
- Dispose of toilet paper with human waste when possible

Handwashing Station:

- Create dedicated handwashing station near toilet area
- Use tippy-tap design if running water unavailable
- Stock with soap and paper towels
- Make mandatory after toilet use and before food handling

During urban disaster response, I worked with an apartment complex that maintained remarkably good health through three weeks without municipal services by implementing a disciplined waste management system using these exact protocols. The community suffered zero cases of dysentery despite surrounding areas experiencing widespread outbreaks.

Personal Hygiene Under Constraints: Preventing Skin and Soft Tissue Infections

When normal bathing becomes difficult, strategic hygiene prevents many common emergency medical issues:

Prioritized Cleaning Protocol:

- Hands: Multiple times daily, especially before food handling and after waste contact
- Face: Daily cleaning prevents eye and respiratory infections
- Feet: Daily inspection and cleaning prevents potentially devastating infections
- Groin and underarms: High priority for infection and com-

fort
- Dental hygiene: Maintains critical first-line immune defense

Water Conservation Techniques:

- Use spray bottles for targeted cleaning
- Implement Navy shower technique (wet, turn off water, soap, rinse briefly)
- Collect and reuse "gray water" for flushing and cleaning
- Use baby wipes for waterless cleaning when necessary

Special Population Considerations:

- Infants: Clean diaper area with each change; use diluted vinegar for diaper rash
- Elderly: Prevent pressure sores through position changes and skin inspection
- Diabetics: Daily foot inspection and cleaning is non-negotiable

I once consulted with a community shelter after a major hurricane where skin infections had affected nearly 30% of residents. By implementing zones of hygiene priority and scheduled cleaning rotations, we reduced new infections to zero within 72 hours despite continuing water restrictions.

Mental Health Triage in Crisis Situations

The psychological impact of disasters frequently outlasts the physical effects. Understanding basic mental health triage principles helps maintain function during extended crises.

Acute Stress Response Management: Maintaining Function

Immediate psychological responses to disaster can compromise decision-making and survival activities:

Recognition Signs:

- Physical: Rapid breathing, elevated heart rate, trembling, nausea
- Cognitive: Difficulty concentrating, confusion, memory lapses
- Emotional: Fear, anxiety, numbness, inappropriate emotions
- Behavioral: Hyperactivity, freezing, argumentativeness, withdrawal

Field Intervention Protocol:

- Apply tactical breathing: 4-count inhale, 4-count hold, 4-count exhale, 4-count hold
- Implement grounding techniques: Identify 5 things you see, 4 things you feel, 3 things you hear, 2 things you smell, 1 thing you taste
- Assign simple, concrete tasks that provide sense of control and accomplishment
- Maintain hydration and blood sugar levels—physiological stability supports psychological stability

Supportive Communication Techniques:

- Use simple, concrete language
- Give clear, actionable directions
- Avoid phrases like "don't worry" or "calm down"

- Acknowledge reality without catastrophizing

During earthquake aftershock sequences, I've guided individuals through acute stress responses by assigning them simple inventory tasks while using tactical breathing. The combination of rhythmic breathing, mental focus, and purposeful activity consistently reduces acute stress symptoms within 10-15 minutes.

Sleep Management: The Foundation of Mental Resilience
Sleep disruption dramatically compromises cognitive function and emotional regulation:

Crisis Sleep Hygiene Protocol:

- Maintain consistent sleep-wake schedule despite irregular conditions
- Create designated sleep area separate from activity spaces
- Reduce light exposure for 1 hour before intended sleep time
- Implement sleep rotation schedule for security watches

Sleep Aid Considerations:

- Antihistamines (Benadryl) can provide short-term assistance but lose effectiveness with continued use
- Melatonin provides more sustainable support for sleep cycle regulation
- Avoid alcohol—it fragments sleep architecture despite sedative effects
- Herbal options include valerian root, chamomile, and lavender

Special Population Accommodations:

- Children: Maintain bedtime routines even in austere conditions
- Elderly: Often require less total sleep but more consistent schedule
- Those with PTSD: May benefit from security measures visible from sleep position

During an extended wildfire evacuation, one shelter leader implemented a remarkably effective sleep protocol that maintained resident functionality despite chaotic conditions. By creating designated quiet hours and sleep spaces, they preserved the cognitive function needed for effective disaster response.

Psychological First Aid: Supporting Emotional Recovery

When professional mental health resources are unavailable, these psychological first aid (PFA) principles support recovery:

Core PFA Actions:

- Promote safety: Physical and psychological security
- Promote calm: Stress management and emotional regulation
- Promote connection: Facilitate social support
- Promote self-efficacy: Encourage active problem-solving
- Promote hope: Identify sources of potential positive outcomes

Communication Techniques:

- Listen more than you speak

- Avoid phrases like "I understand" or "I know how you feel"
- Validate emotions without judgment
- Focus on present needs rather than past losses
- Recognize cultural differences in emotional expression

Red Flag Recognition:

- Expressions of hopelessness or worthlessness
- Talk of being a burden to others
- Increasing withdrawal from group activities
- Giving away possessions
- Sudden mood improvement after depression

During a protracted urban crisis, I helped implement a community mental health monitoring system using these principles. The system identified several high-risk individuals who received peer support interventions that likely prevented suicide attempts during the extended isolation period.

Emergency Medical Assessment Flow Chart

When facing medical emergencies without professional assistance, this systematic assessment protocol guides response priorities and intervention decisions. This is your roadmap through the most common crisis medical scenarios.

IMMEDIATE LIFE THREAT ASSESSMENT

Is the scene safe for approach?

- **NO** → Secure scene or establish safe extraction plan before proceeding
- **YES** → Proceed to next step

Is the person responsive?

- **NO** → Open airway (head tilt/chin lift), check breathing for 10 seconds
- Not breathing or only gasping → Begin CPR if trained
- Breathing normally → Place in recovery position, monitor
- **YES** → Proceed to next step

Is there severe bleeding?

- **YES** → Apply direct pressure and elevate limb
- If bleeding continues → Apply pressure to appropriate arterial pressure point
- If bleeding still continues → Apply tourniquet as last resort
- **NO** → Proceed to next step

Are there signs of shock? (Rapid pulse, pale/clammy skin, confusion)

- **YES** → Elevate legs, maintain body temperature, provide small sips of water if conscious
- **NO** → Proceed to full assessment

SECONDARY ASSESSMENT PROTOCOL

Check vital signs if possible:

- Normal adult ranges:
- Pulse: 60-100 beats per minute
- Respirations: 12-20 breaths per minute
- BP (if equipment available): 90-140/60-90 mmHg

Perform head-to-toe examination:

- Head: Check for wounds, depressions, fluid from ears/nose
- Neck: Check for deformity, tenderness, abnormal veins
- Chest: Check for equal rise/fall, wounds, breathing difficulty
- Abdomen: Check for tenderness, rigidity, distension
- Pelvis: Check for stability, deformity, bleeding
- Extremities: Check for deformity, circulation, sensation, movement
- Back: Check for deformity, wounds, tenderness

Obtain SAMPLE history if person is responsive:

- **S**: Signs/Symptoms (What's wrong?)
- **A**: Allergies (Any medical allergies?)
- **M**: Medications (What medications do you take?)
- **P**: Past medical history (Any medical conditions?)
- **L**: Last intake (When did you last eat or drink?)
- **E**: Events leading to illness/injury (What happened?)

SPECIFIC CONDITION MANAGEMENT

HEAT EMERGENCIES:

- Heat exhaustion (heavy sweating, weakness, normal mental status)
- Move to cool area, remove excess clothing, apply cool wet cloths
- Give sips of water if fully conscious
- Heat stroke (hot dry skin, altered mental status)

91

- Immediately cool body by any means available
- Do not give oral fluids
- URGENT: Cool first, transport second

COLD EMERGENCIES:

- Frostbite (white/grayish skin, numbness, waxy feel)
- Do not rub affected area
- Warm gradually with body heat or warm (not hot) water
- Do not rewarm if refreezing is possible
- Hypothermia (shivering, confusion, drowsiness)
- Remove wet clothing, warm core first
- Use available heat sources and insulation
- Give warm sweet drinks if fully conscious

ALLERGIC REACTIONS:

- Mild (localized itching, rash)
- Antihistamine if available, monitor for progression
- Severe (difficulty breathing, face/throat swelling)
- Administer epinephrine auto-injector if available
- Help into position of comfort, typically sitting
- Monitor closely for deterioration

DIABETIC EMERGENCIES:

- Low blood sugar (confusion, weakness, seizure)
- If conscious: Give sugar source (juice, honey, glucose tablets)
- If unconscious: Do not give oral substances
- High blood sugar (excessive thirst, frequent urination,

fruity breath)
- Give water if conscious, avoid further sugar intake
- Monitor for deterioration of consciousness

SEIZURES:

- Protect from injury: Remove hazards, cushion head
- Do not restrain or put anything in mouth
- Time seizure duration
- After seizure, place in recovery position
- Medical attention necessary for first-time seizure or seizure lasting >5 minutes

WOUND MANAGEMENT DECISION TREE

Is the wound bleeding severely?

- **YES** → Control bleeding before proceeding
- **NO** → Proceed to next step

Is there an embedded object?

- **YES** → Do not remove; stabilize object and dress around it
- **NO** → Proceed to next step

Is the wound heavily contaminated?

- **YES** → Irrigate thoroughly before considering closure
- **NO** → Proceed to next step

Is the wound:

- Less than 8 hours old, clean, and with edges that close easily
- Consider closure with butterfly bandages or similar
- Older than 8 hours, heavily contaminated, or edges don't close easily
- Leave open, cover with moist dressing, change daily

After initial treatment:

- Monitor for infection signs: increasing pain, redness, swelling, warmth, pus
- Redress daily using clean technique
- Elevate injured extremities when possible

This flow chart guides initial response and basic management. It's not a substitute for professional medical care but can bridge the gap until such care becomes available. Implementing these protocols can prevent a manageable emergency from becoming a life-threatening crisis.

When professional help arrives, provide clear, concise information about your assessment findings and the care you've provided. This information transfer is as important as the care itself, as it guides continuing treatment decisions that may significantly impact long-term outcomes.

6

Surviving When the Grid Fails

When the lights go out, modern humans typically do two things: check if the neighbors' power is also out, then immediately reach for their phones to search "power outage in my area." This instinctive digital response reveals just how thoroughly we've forgotten what our grandparents knew intuitively—how to function when the power grid fails.

I've been on-site during extended blackouts across five continents, from ice storms in rural New England to infrastructure collapse in former Soviet republics. The pattern is remarkably consistent: the first 24 hours are characterized by optimistic waiting, the next 48 by growing frustration, and beyond that, either adaptation or increasingly desperate attempts to maintain an unsustainable normal.

The difference between these outcomes isn't wealth, property size, or even initial supply levels. It's knowledge and adaptability. I've watched wealthy homeowners with 5,000-square-foot houses become effectively homeless within days of grid failure while neighboring families in modest ranches created functional microcosms of civilization using repurposed household items and systematic energy management.

This chapter isn't about building an off-grid paradise with equipment you don't have time to acquire. It's about leveraging what already exists on-site in your home within 48 hours! It's about creating functional power alternatives, managing your limited energy resources, and establishing safe illumination, communication, and climate control when the infrastructure you've relied on disappears without warning.

Remember: humans thrived for thousands of years without the electrical grid. Your great-grandparents knew how to live this way. It's not about primitive survival—it's about rediscovering practical knowledge that's been obscured by convenience.

Immediate Power Alternatives with Household Items

When the grid fails, your home still contains numerous potential energy sources hiding in plain sight. The key is identifying and leveraging them systematically before they're depleted or damaged.

Extracting Maximum Value from Vehicle Electrical Systems

Your vehicle represents one of your most accessible and powerful energy reserves during a crisis:

Basic Vehicle Power Utilization:

- Car batteries provide 12V DC power capable of charging phones, laptops, and small devices
- Use a car USB adapter or inverter to convert to usable power
- Run the engine for 10 minutes every hour of charging to prevent battery depletion
- Position vehicle outdoors or with garage door fully open to prevent carbon monoxide poisoning

Advanced Vehicle Battery Integration:

- Connect a power inverter directly to the battery terminals for higher-power applications
- Use jumper cables to connect vehicle battery to deep-cycle batteries for power transfer
- For hybrid vehicles, activate "utility mode" if available for extended power generation
- Remember that most vehicles can produce 500-1500 watts while running, exceeding typical portable power stations

During a week-long ice storm outage, a family powered critical medical equipment using their minivan's electrical system. By running the vehicle for 20 minutes every two hours and using a quality inverter, they maintained essential life support with minimal fuel consumption. The key was systematic management rather than continuous operation.

Unconventional Battery Harvesting

Your home contains dozens of overlooked battery sources that can be repurposed during emergencies:

Consolidation Protocol:

- Gather all battery-powered devices: toys, tools, rarely-used electronics
- Standardize by battery type: AA, AAA, C, D, 9V, button cells
- Extract batteries using proper technique to prevent damage
- Test and sort by remaining capacity using a battery tester or device with power indicator

Device Battery Repurposing:

- Laptop batteries: Most contain multiple lithium cells that can be carefully extracted
- Power tool batteries: Provide 12-20V of high-amperage power when adapted
- UPS systems: Contains sealed lead-acid batteries that function like smaller car batteries
- Electric scooters/bikes: Often contain high-capacity lithium batteries ideal for powering small electronics

Battery Combination Techniques:

- Series connection (positive to negative): Increases voltage
- Parallel connection (positive to positive, negative to negative): Increases capacity/runtime
- Use aluminum foil as emergency battery contact material
- Secure connections with electrical or duct tape

I once assisted a family during an urban power outage who powered an emergency radio for two weeks using batteries harvested from household devices they'd forgotten they owned. By systematically collecting and deploying these resources, they maintained critical information access long after their neighbors had exhausted commercial battery supplies.

Solar Harvesting Without Solar Panels

While dedicated solar systems are ideal, improvised solar harvesting can provide meaningful power:

Passive Solar Device Charging:

- Place dark-colored containers of water in direct sunlight
- Position small electronics on these solar-heated surfaces
- Battery efficiency improves significantly at optimal temper-

atures (68-77°F/20-25°C)

- This method can extend battery life by 15-30% in cold conditions

Improvised Solar Collectors:

- Aluminum foil arranged in parabolic shape can concentrate sunlight
- Position phone/device at focal point for accelerated solar heating
- Outdated CDs/DVDs can serve as reflective concentrators
- Car windshield reflectors can be repurposed as solar collectors

Small-Scale Solar Options:

- Solar garden lights contain small photovoltaic cells and rechargeable batteries
- Calculator solar cells can trickle-charge small capacitors or batteries
- Solar-powered toys can be disassembled for their components
- Even small smartphone solar chargers can maintain critical communication capability

During disaster response work in Puerto Rico, communities used improvised solar concentrators to maintain the charge in essential communication devices when conventional charging became impossible. While slow, these methods provided sufficient power to maintain emergency contact capabilities.

Battery Prioritization and Management

Not all battery-powered devices are equally important, and not all batteries should be deployed simultaneously. Strategic allocation of limited battery resources dramatically extends your functional capability during extended outages.

Device Criticality Assessment

Evaluate your battery-powered devices using this hierarchy of need:

Tier 1: Life-Critical Systems

- Medical devices: Oxygen concentrators, CPAP machines, medication refrigeration
- Security systems: Perimeter alarms, motion detectors
- Critical environmental controls: Carbon monoxide detectors, smoke alarms
- Essential communication: Single designated emergency communication device

Tier 2: Functional Maintenance Systems

- Primary lighting solutions
- Weather monitoring equipment
- Additional communication devices
- Information resources (radios, small media devices)

Tier 3: Comfort and Convenience

- Secondary lighting
- Entertainment devices
- Comfort-focused devices
- Labor-saving tools

During a regional outage, I consulted with a neighborhood that implemented a ruthless device prioritization system. By dedicating their highest-quality batteries exclusively to tier-one devices and systematically downgrading depleted batteries to lower-tier applications, they maintained critical functions for nearly three weeks—far longer than communities that distributed battery resources uniformly across all devices.

Battery Life Extension Techniques

These methods can extend battery functionality beyond normal expectations:

Temperature Management:

- Store batteries at temperatures between 40-80°F (4-27°C)
- Warm cold batteries before use (pocket carry for 30 minutes)
- Prevent exposure to temperature extremes, especially heat
- Insulate battery-powered devices during cold weather use

Discharge Management:

- Implement strict duty cycles: 1 hour use / 3 hours rest extends overall function
- Remove batteries from devices when not in use
- Use batteries until full depletion in non-critical applications
- Match battery capacity to device requirements (don't use high-capacity batteries in low-drain devices)

Recovery Techniques:

- "Dead" alkaline batteries often recover partial capacity after 24-48 hours of rest

- Warming alkaline batteries to 100°F (38°C) can temporarily restore function
- Tapping or rotating batteries can redistribute electrolyte and extend function
- For multi-cell devices, rotating battery positions can extend overall function

During winter storm response, a community health center extended their emergency battery supplies by nearly 40% by implementing strict temperature management and systematic rotation protocols. The batteries didn't last longer—they extracted more functional capacity from each battery through systematic management.

Emergency Battery Charging Methods

When conventional charging becomes impossible, these methods can restore partial function:

Mechanical Charging Systems:

- Hand-crank generators (often found in emergency radios)
- Bicycle generators (some exercise bikes can be converted)
- Pull-cord generators (similar to lawnmower starters)
- Water wheel generators (for properties with flowing water)

Thermal Charging Methods:

- Thermoelectric generators using temperature differential
- Place certain batteries in sealed bags in freezer before power loss
- Chemical reaction charging systems (typically zinc-carbon)
- Apply careful heat to rechargeable batteries (specific types

only)

Improvised Charging Systems:

- Lemon/potato battery concept for small electronics
- Solar trickle-charging using small cells in parallel
- Wind-up watch mechanisms connected to small generators
- Motion-harvesting systems from swinging pendulums

I've worked with rural communities who maintained emergency communication capability for weeks using only mechanical charging methods. While labor-intensive, these approaches provided sufficient power to maintain essential functions when all conventional options had failed.

Safe Emergency Lighting Methods

Light isn't just about convenience—it's about safety and psychological well-being. Extended darkness dramatically increases accident rates and significantly impacts mental health. Strategic illumination preserves both.

Lighting Efficiency Hierarchy

Not all lighting methods are equally efficient. Prioritize your options according to this hierarchy:

LED Technology:

- Most efficient light source available (up to 100 lumens per watt)
- Headlamps provide directed light while keeping hands free
- LED lanterns offer better area illumination
- LED flashlights provide focused illumination for specific tasks

- Battery life typically 20-50 hours on low settings

Chemical Light Sources:

- Lightsticks provide 6-12 hours of moderate area illumination
- No heat production or fire risk
- Can be "paused" by placing in freezer or cold area
- Multiple colors available, with green typically providing highest efficiency
- Single-use only, but excellent shelf life (2-4 years)

Fuel-Based Light Sources:

- Liquid fuel lanterns (white gas, kerosene) provide bright illumination but require ventilation
- Candles offer 8-12 hours per inch of taper, but present fire risk
- Oil lamps using vegetable, mineral, or lamp oil
- Canned heat products (Sterno) can provide both light and heat

I once consulted with a mountain community during a winter-long isolation period. By implementing a strict progression from high-efficiency LEDs to fuel-based options as batteries depleted, they maintained functional illumination for nearly three months despite having initial supplies designed for only three weeks.

Strategic Illumination Deployment

Lighting every space as you did with grid power is impossible and unnecessary. Implement this strategic approach:

Zone-Based Lighting Protocol:

- Operational zones: Areas where tasks are being performed (cooking, repair work)
- Transition zones: Hallways, stairwells, pathways between functional areas
- Safety zones: Bathrooms, areas with hazards
- Sleeping zones: Minimal illumination required

Illumination Scheduling:

- Full lighting: Only during essential operations
- Reduced lighting: During evening gathering times
- Pathway lighting: During nighttime navigation
- Darkness: Maximize during sleeping hours to conserve resources

Light Source Selection by Zone:

- Task lighting: Focused light sources (headlamps, flashlights)
- Area lighting: Diffuse light sources (lanterns)
- Pathway lighting: Low-level continuous sources (solar garden lights brought indoors)
- Emergency lighting: Readily accessible, known-good sources for unexpected needs

During extended urban outages, families who created zone-based lighting protocols typically maintained functional illumination 3-5 times longer than those attempting to maintain whole-house lighting. The efficiency difference is substantial.

Improvised Light Sources and Amplification

When conventional lighting options are depleted, these improvised alternatives can provide critical illumination:

Emergency Candle Alternatives:

- Crayons (remove paper, light thick end, burns 30+ minutes)
- Vegetable oil lamps using metal containers and cotton wicks
- Butter lamps using small containers and cotton string
- Citrus peel oil lamps (orange/lemon peels filled with vegetable oil)

Light Amplification Techniques:

- Strategic mirror placement to multiply available light
- Aluminum foil reflectors behind light sources
- Water bottles as light diffusers and magnifiers
- White sheets hung as wall coverings to increase reflectivity

Ambient Light Utilization:

- Position activities to maximize natural light during daylight
- Use reflective materials to direct light into darker areas
- Arrange sleeping areas to leverage moonlight when available
- Remove window coverings during day, replace before dark

During disaster response in developing regions, remarkable improvised lighting systems have been created from discarded materials. One particularly effective design used water-filled clear bottles installed through metal roofing to refract daylight into otherwise dark structures. Creativity often outperforms technology when resources are constrained.

Communication Options When Networks Fail

When cellular networks and internet service fail, maintaining communication becomes both more challenging and more critical. Understanding your options beyond conventional networks provides essential connectivity during extended emergencies.

Radio Communication Systems

Radio provides the most reliable emergency communication framework:

Weather Radio Monitoring:

- NOAA Weather Radio (162.400-162.550 MHz) provides emergency broadcasts
- Battery-powered weather radios often include hand-crank charging
- Program to receive Emergency Alert System notifications
- Establish regular monitoring schedule to preserve batteries

Two-Way Radio Options:

- Family Radio Service (FRS) radios: 0.5-2 mile practical range
- General Mobile Radio Service (GMRS) radios: 2-5 mile range (license required)
- Citizen's Band (CB) radios: Vehicle-mounted units provide 3-10 mile range
- Amateur (Ham) Radio: Extensive capabilities but requires

licensing

Improvised Antenna Enhancements:

- Attach metal coat hangers to existing antennas
- Copper wire extensions in straight-line configuration
- Aluminum foil reflecting panels behind radios
- Elevation improvements (operating from second floors or higher)

During hurricane recovery operations, I coordinated with a neighborhood network using basic FRS radios. By establishing centralized message relay protocols and deploying simple antenna improvements, they maintained communication across a three-mile area despite complete infrastructure failure.

Non-Electronic Communication Methods

When all electronic options fail, these systems provide functional alternatives:

Visual Signaling Systems:

- Window signals using colored paper/fabric
- Flag systems with pre-established meanings
- Light signals using Morse code or simple patterns
- Reflective signaling using mirrors during daylight

Community Bulletin Locations:

- Centralized information boards at community gathering points
- Message drop locations for non-urgent communications

- Runner systems for critical messages
- Regular in-person briefings at established times and locations

Sound-Based Communication:

- Whistle patterns for emergency alerting
- Car horn sequences for neighborhood notifications
- Bell or percussion instruments for community alerts
- Voice amplification using simple megaphones

I've worked with mountain communities that maintained effective emergency communication during extended winter isolations using nothing but visual signals and daily messenger routes. Their success stemmed not from technical sophistication but from clear pre-established protocols and disciplined implementation.

Power Conservation for Critical Devices

When communication devices depend on irreplaceable battery power, these techniques extend functionality:

Device Management Protocol:

- Designate one device as the primary emergency communicator
- Turn off all non-essential features (Bluetooth, WiFi, location services)
- Reduce screen brightness to minimum usable level
- Schedule specific communication windows rather than remaining continuously available

Messaging Efficiency:

- Use text-based communication rather than voice when possible
- Establish communication schedules to avoid repeated connection attempts
- Create standardized message formats to reduce composition time
- Use group messaging to reduce repetitive communications

Signal Optimization:

- Identify locations with strongest remaining signal
- Create signal maps marking functional communication points
- Elevate devices for improved reception
- Use vehicle-mounted antennas when available

During wildfire evacuations in the western United States, I advised several neighborhood groups on emergency communication protocols. Those who implemented strict device management and established clear communication windows maintained critical connectivity for 7-10 days on battery resources that would typically have been exhausted in 48 hours under normal usage patterns.

Heat and Cooking Without Electricity or Gas

Temperature regulation—both for your living space and your food—becomes an immediate challenge when conventional energy sources fail. Understanding alternative heating and cooking methods allows you to maintain both comfort and nutrition.

Emergency Heating Hierarchy

When conventional heating fails, implement these alternatives in order of safety and efficiency:

Existing Alternative Systems:

- Wood stoves and fireplaces (ensure proper ventilation)
- Kerosene heaters (requires adequate ventilation, carbon monoxide detection)
- Propane space heaters rated for indoor use
- Catalytic heaters with low-oxygen shutoff protection

Space Isolation and Heat Conservation:

- Reduce heated space to minimum necessary area
- Create internal room within room using suspended blankets
- Use plastic sheeting to seal unused areas
- Deploy weather stripping and door sweeps to prevent heat loss

Body-Centric Heating Approaches:

- Layer clothing using technical principles (moisture-wicking base, insulating mid, wind/water resistant outer)
- Use emergency blankets (Mylar) as clothing liners and bed insulation
- Create shared warming areas utilizing body heat from multiple people
- Implement activity rotation to generate body heat at regular intervals

During a severe ice storm that left temperatures below freezing in homes for over a week, I worked with elderly residents who maintained survivable conditions by creating "microenvironments" within their homes. By isolating single rooms with hanging blankets and focusing on body-centric heat management, they maintained 60°F+ (15°C+) temperatures despite exterior walls dropping to freezing temperatures.

Alternative Cooking Methods

Food preparation without conventional energy requires both alternative heat sources and adapted cooking techniques:

Non-Electric Cooking Appliances:

- Camp stoves (propane, liquid fuel, solid fuel)
- Charcoal or wood grills (outdoor use only)
- Rocket stoves using small wood pieces
- Solar ovens (weather-dependent but zero-fuel operation)

Improvised Cooking Systems:

- Buddy burners (tuna can, cardboard, wax)
- Hobo stoves (ventilated metal cans)
- Brick rocket stoves
- Dakota fire holes (outdoor, underground fire management)

Fuel-Free Cooking Techniques:

- Cold soaking (rehydrating food without heat)
- Chemical cooking (MRE-style heating packs)
- Hay box/retained heat cooking
- Solar cooking using reflective materials

During post-hurricane recovery operations, communities have developed remarkably efficient cooking systems using minimal resources. One particularly effective approach combined brief active cooking on rocket stoves with hay box heat retention, allowing complete meal preparation while using only 20% of the fuel normally required.

Food Selection for Energy Efficiency

When energy for cooking becomes limited, food selection must adapt accordingly:

Cooking Efficiency Categories:

- No-cook foods: Ready to eat without preparation
- Minimum-cook foods: Brief heating or hot water addition only
- Efficient-cook foods: Quick-cooking items that require minimal fuel
- Extended-cook foods: Reserve for specific situations with adequate fuel

Energy-Optimized Meal Planning:

- Plan one hot meal daily rather than three
- Combine multiple cooking needs during single heating session
- Precook and reheat rather than cooking from raw state each time
- Use insulated containers to retain heat during cooking process

Preparation Method Adaptation:

- Convert boiling recipes to simmering to reduce fuel use
- Implement small-batch cooking rather than large-pot methods
- Pre-soak grains and beans to reduce cooking time by 50%+
- Finely chop ingredients to speed cooking time

I once advised a large evacuation shelter on cooking system optimization after supply lines were disrupted. By implementing energy-efficient food selection and preparation methods, they reduced fuel consumption by approximately 70% while still providing hot food to all residents at least once daily.

The Blackout Survival Sequence

When the grid fails, the actions you take in the first 60 minutes dramatically impact your resilience over the subsequent days or weeks. This sequence provides the optimal response pattern based on observed outcomes across multiple extended outages.

0-15 MINUTES: IMMEDIATE RESPONSE

Power Assessment:

- Check circuit breakers/fuses to determine if outage is internal or external
- Observe neighborhood indicators (street lights, other homes)
- Check power company app/website using cellular data
- Set outage alert notifications if system still accessible

Device Preservation:

- Unplug sensitive electronics (computers, TVs) to prevent

surge damage
- Place network devices (modem, router) on definitive off position
- Set mobile devices to low-power mode immediately
- Turn off and unplug major appliances to prevent surge damage on restoration

Resource Inventory:

- Locate all flashlights and confirm functionality
- Identify all device charging options currently available
- Account for all household members and brief on situation
- Assess current alternative light/heat/cooking resources

Communication Establishment:

- Designate primary and backup communication devices
- Make critical notifications while communication is still reliable
- Download any essential information while internet is potentially accessible
- Establish check-in protocol with family/neighbors

15-30 MINUTES: STABILIZATION
Light Source Deployment:

- Distribute light sources to strategic locations
- Implement zone lighting protocol
- Establish nighttime pathway illumination
- Set up primary activity area with appropriate lighting

Power Conservation Implementation:

- Turn off all non-essential battery devices
- Collect all potential battery sources into central location
- Deploy power banks to maximum charge if grid still unavailable
- Establish device charging priority list

Critical Systems Backup:

- Check status of medical devices and implement backup power
- Verify security system backup functionality
- Assess sump pump/basement flood risk if applicable
- Implement refrigeration preservation protocol

Information Gathering:

- Use vehicle radio for emergency broadcasts
- Check NOAA weather radio for situation updates
- Communicate with neighbors about local impacts
- Assess expected outage duration if information available

30-45 MINUTES: ENVIRONMENT PREPARATION

Temperature Management:

- Implement appropriate heating/cooling strategy based on season
- Close blinds/curtains for insulation
- Adjust clothing for anticipated temperature changes

- Consolidate household members in optimal temperature zone

Water Security:

- Fill containers with drinking water while pressure remains
- Fill bathtub for non-potable water needs
- Turn off water main if freeze risk or contamination risk exists
- Identify alternative water sources if outage extends

Food System Adaptation:

- Inventory refrigerator contents and prioritize consumption
- Organize no-cook meal options
- Prepare cooling strategy for refrigerated items
- Set up alternative cooking method if extended outage expected

Sanitation Preparation:

- Flush toilets to completely fill tanks while pressure exists
- Prepare alternative toilet options if water-dependent systems may fail
- Set up handwashing station with minimal water requirements
- Prepare gray water collection for toilet flushing

45-60 MINUTES: EXTENDED PREPARATION

Sleep System Preparation:

117

- Organize appropriate bedding for anticipated temperatures
- Establish sleeping areas in temperature-optimal locations
- Prepare sleep system insulation from below (critical for heat retention)
- Deploy chemical hand/foot warmers inside bedding if cold conditions

Safety Enhancement:

- Place battery-powered lighting at tripping hazard locations
- Verify smoke/CO detector functionality
- Stage fire extinguisher in appropriate location
- Secure any hazards that may be less visible in reduced lighting

Community Integration:

- Check on vulnerable neighbors if appropriate
- Establish resource-sharing arrangements if beneficial
- Coordinate neighborhood information gathering
- Develop mutual aid systems for extended outages

Psychological Preparation:

- Set expectations for outage duration (typically 2-3× initial estimates)
- Brief household on conservation protocols
- Establish regular situation review schedule
- Organize morale-maintaining activities that don't require power

This sequence reflects lessons learned from dozens of extended power outages across varied environments. The structured approach prevents the scattered, reactive response that typically characterizes the initial phase of sudden grid failure and establishes a functional alternative system before battery-powered devices are depleted.

The grid-independent lifestyle isn't a primitive regression— it's the normal human condition throughout most of history. Your great-grandparents navigated daily life without the power infrastructure you've come to depend on. Their knowledge hasn't become irrelevant; it's simply been buried under layers of convenience. Excavate it now, while you still can.

7

Self-Defense and Security - Protecting What You Have

The most dangerous survival myth I've encountered is that desperate people behave like movie villains—announcing their intentions, making dramatic threats, and giving you time to deliver clever one-liners before you defend yourself. Having worked in collapsed economies and post-disaster zones, I can tell you with absolute certainty: real-world security threats don't monologue before attacking.

In actual crisis situations, predatory behavior is typically opportunistic, silent, and brutally efficient. The home invasion you might be visualizing—the midnight standoff with armed intruders where you heroically defend your castle—is extraordinarily rare compared to the much more common scenario: someone quietly observing your patterns, identifying vulnerabilities, and striking during momentary lapses in awareness.

I've interviewed hundreds of survivors who experienced property crimes during disasters. The consistent pattern isn't dramatic confrontation but the quiet shock of realizing someone has been watching, waiting, and exploiting predictable behaviors. The family that maintains rigid routines, the house with obvious indicators of preparedness, the shelter with visible resources but minimal security awareness—these become targets not through random chance but through the predatory calculus of opportunity versus risk.

This chapter isn't about turning you into an action hero. It's about reducing your target profile, increasing the perceived difficulty of victimizing you, and implementing practical security measures using materials you already possess. We'll focus on awareness first, deterrence second, and direct defense as an absolute last resort. Because in real-world crisis scenarios, the confrontation you avoid is infinitely more survivable than the one you "win."

Situational Awareness in Crisis Environments

The foundation of all effective security is awareness. Your ability to detect threats before they materialize gives you crucial response time and often allows you to avoid danger entirely. Crisis environments dramatically change the threat landscape in ways that require immediate adaptation of your awareness patterns.

The Awareness Hierarchy: Observe, Orient, Decide, Act

The OODA Loop (Observe, Orient, Decide, Act) provides a structured framework for situational awareness that can be implemented immediately:

Observe: Actively scan your environment for anomalies

- Implement the 30/30 rule: Every 30 seconds, scan 30 feet in all directions
- Categorize observations as normal, unusual, or threatening
- Pay particular attention to repeated patterns or individuals

· Maintain awareness of exit routes and defensive positions

Orient: Interpret observations through crisis-appropriate filters

· Understand that normal social constraints have weakened
· Recognize that resource scarcity changes behavioral norms
· Adjust threat thresholds based on specific crisis context
· Interpret behavior patterns, not just individual actions

Decide: Determine appropriate response to potential threats

· Match response to threat level (avoid, deter, defend)
· Consider consequences of each potential action
· Establish decision triggers for specific scenarios
· Maintain decision discipline—emotional responses decrease survivability

Act: Implement your decision with appropriate intensity

· Move with purpose but without panic
· Communicate clearly with family/group members
· Execute practiced responses rather than improvising
· Maintain awareness throughout action implementation

During the aftermath of Hurricane Katrina, I observed groups using formalized observation protocols—assigning specific observation sectors and implementing regular reporting requirements. Their systematic approach identified potential threats significantly earlier than the casual observation patterns typical of most groups, allowing proactive rather than reactive security responses.

Baseline Mapping: Detecting What Doesn't Belong

Establishing environmental baselines allows you to quickly identify anomalies that may represent threats:

Environmental Baseline Establishment:

- Document normal activity patterns in your area
- Note regular visitors, vehicles, and schedule patterns
- Identify normal noise levels and types
- Map typical movement flows and gathering points

Active Anomaly Detection:

- New individuals observing your location
- Changes in traffic or pedestrian patterns
- Unusual silence or noise
- Abandoned vehicles or recently discarded items
- Repeated "coincidental" encounters with the same individuals

Pattern Recognition Focus:

- Multiple sightings of the same individual/vehicle in different locations
- Individuals with inappropriate dress for weather/location
- Forced casualness or avoidance of eye contact
- Activities that don't match stated or apparent purposes
- Photography or observation of security features

During civil unrest, a neighborhood association maintained a communal anomaly log. Each household documented unusual observations, which were consolidated daily. This approach repeatedly identified pattern-based threats that would have been dismissed as isolated incidents by individual observers. Collective awareness exponentially increases security effectiveness.

The Gray Man Concept: Strategic Invisibility

In crisis environments, visibility often equals vulnerability. The "gray man" approach focuses on reducing your profile as a potential target:

Appearance Management:

- Adopt mid-range clothing that doesn't suggest either wealth or destitution
- Avoid tactical gear, preparedness-related clothing, or obvious indicators of resources
- Match general appearance to prevailing community standard
- Remove logos, brands, and identifiers that suggest specific affiliations or resources

Behavioral Blending:

- Mirror the pace, posture, and general demeanor of those around you
- Avoid behaviors that draw attention (loud conversations, arguing)
- Implement subdued observation techniques that don't reveal your awareness level
- Practice the "middle path" in all behaviors—neither the

most confident nor the most fearful

Resource Concealment:

- Transport supplies in generic, non-descriptive containers
- Conduct resource management activities away from public observation
- Develop cover stories for necessary movements and activities
- Create disinformation through controlled information release when necessary

During long-term food shortages in an urban environment, there are families who maintained adequate supplies while experiencing no security incidents. Their consistent approach involved complete avoidance of behaviors that would indicate preparedness—no visible stockpiles, no discussions of supplies, and careful management of waste that might reveal consumption patterns different from the surrounding community.

Home Defense with Non-Traditional Tools

When traditional security options are unavailable, ordinary household items can be repurposed to create effective defensive systems. The key is understanding security from first principles rather than relying on conventional products.

Perimeter Alert Systems Using Household Items

Early warning provides crucial response time. These systems create effective alerts using common materials:

External Noise Generators:

- Wind chimes positioned at entry paths and access points

- Aluminum cans containing small rocks suspended from fishing line
- Metal baking sheets loosely stacked where movement will disturb them
- Glass bottles arranged to roll or fall when disturbed

Trip Wire Configurations:

- Fishing line connected to noise-generating objects
- Thin wire positioned at ankle height across likely approach paths
- Monofilament strung with bells or metal objects
- Holiday decorations repurposed as alert systems

Motion Detection Enhancements:

- Mirrors positioned to extend sightlines from observation points
- Battery-powered motion sensor lights from home decor/-closet applications
- Pet toys with motion-activated sounds
- Solar garden lights positioned to create shadow anomalies when paths are crossed

During a prolonged winter power outage, a rural community improvised alert systems around isolated homes. The most effective approach involved multiple layers of notification, with subtle early warning systems at distance (for awareness) and more obvious systems near entry points (for deterrence). This layered approach provided crucial response time while simultaneously communicating security awareness to potential threats.

Access Control Without Commercial Security

Controlling access to your space creates both physical and psychological barriers to intrusion:

Entry Point Hardening:

- Door reinforcement using 2×4 lumber in brackets or floor holes
- Hinges secured with 3-inch screws extending into structural framing
- Windows secured with removable cross-bars (tension-mounted curtain rods)
- Pet doors and other alternative entries permanently secured

Psychological Deterrents:

- Security signage (even without active systems)
- Visible but controlled lighting suggesting occupancy
- Evidence of activity and awareness
- Indicators of community connection and mutual observation

Delay Mechanisms:

- Furniture arranged to create obstacle course approaches to valuable areas
- Multiple barrier layers requiring distinct breach methods
- Sequential obstacles that make silent entry impossible
- Funneling designs that eliminate multiple-person entry

During civil unrest following a natural disaster, residents of a multi-family apartment building implemented a comprehensive access control system using entirely repurposed materials. Their approach focused on creating multiple delay layers rather than a single "unbreachable" barrier. The time and noise required to navigate their system effectively deterred opportunistic threats while providing occupants with crucial response time.

Defensive Positions Within the Home

If perimeter security fails, interior defensive positions become your final layer of protection:

Safe Room Fundamentals:

- Interior room with minimal entry points
- Solid wood or metal door with reinforced hinges and strike plate
- Communication capability (emergency radio, cell signal)
- Basic sustenance supplies (water, food, medication, sanitation)

Improvised Safe Room Enhancement:

- Furniture barricades positioned for rapid deployment
- Secondary barriers securing vulnerable points (closets, adjoining rooms)
- Planned escape route if safe room is compromised
- Alternative communication methods if primary systems fail

Defensive Position Characteristics:

- Clear fields of observation covering likely approach paths
- Multiple exit options when possible
- Position security from multiple angles
- Concealment from exterior observation

I once advised a family during a civil emergency on converting an interior bathroom into an effective safe room. By removing the existing hollow door and replacing it with a solid exterior door from elsewhere in the house, adding 3-inch screws to secure the hinges and strike plate to the structural framing, and positioning a heavy dresser for rapid barricade deployment, they created a secure space that successfully deterred an intrusion attempt during the third week of the crisis.

Improvised Weapons and Deterrents

In crisis situations, conventional weapons may be unavailable, illegal in your jurisdiction, or impractical for your specific circumstances. Understanding improvised options provides tactical flexibility while maintaining defensive capability.

Distance Maintenance Tools

Creating and maintaining distance from threats is the foundation of personal security:

Reach Extension Implements:

- Broom or mop handles (approximately 4-5 feet of standoff distance)
- Kitchen implements attached to handles (spatulas, ladles)
- Sports equipment (baseball bats, hockey sticks, golf clubs)
- Curtain rods, dowels, or similar rigid items

Barrier Development Materials:

- Furniture positioned to create obstacle courses
- Sheets/blankets suspended to obscure movement and create entanglements
- Slippery substances applied to floors (soapy water, cooking oil)
- Visual barriers that prevent threat targeting

Active Deterrent Options:

- Wasp/hornet spray (legally defensible non-weapon with 20+ foot range)
- Fire extinguisher discharge for visual obstruction
- Garden sprayer filled with vinegar solution
- Improvised riot shield from trash can lid or similar material

During urban riots, a shopkeeper successfully deterred looters using a simple combination of a fire extinguisher discharge followed by a broom handle used to maintain distance. This non-lethal approach effectively protected his property without escalating to potentially lethal confrontation, allowing him to maintain both ethical and legal defensibility in his actions.

Impact Force Multipliers

When distance maintenance fails, these common items can effectively increase defensive impact:

Swinging Impact Tools:

- Rolled magazines secured with tape (surprisingly effective impact tool)
- Sock or small bag filled with coins or batteries
- Flashlights with sturdy construction (particularly tactical

models)
- Kitchen implements with weight at striking end

Fixed Impact Implements:

- Hammer, mallet, or similar tools
- Cast iron cookware
- Heavy doorstops or bookends
- Tools with concentrated impact surfaces

Improvised Defensive Accessories:

- Books or magazines as body armor inserts
- Leather belts wrapped around forearms for limited protection
- Trash can lids or serving trays as shield analogs
- Multiple clothing layers to reduce impact and abrasion injuries

During extended civil unrest in South America, numerous cases where prepared individuals effectively defended themselves using common household items as defensive tools were documented. The most important factor wasn't the specific implement but the psychological commitment to decisive action when necessary, combined with the awareness to prevent most confrontations from occurring in the first place.

Psychological Deterrents and Deception

Often more effective than physical tools, psychological deterrents prevent confrontations before they begin:

Presence Projection:

- Create impression of multiple occupants through varied lighting patterns
- Use different voices during communications (even recorded or imitated)
- Maintain evidence of capacity beyond actual resources
- Deploy male footwear/clothing indicators even in female-only households

Capability Suggestion:

- Visible security indicators (even without actual systems)
- Evidence of awareness and preparedness
- "Beware of dog" signage regardless of pet presence
- Indication of community connection and mutual defense arrangements

Strategic Misdirection:

- Visible "decoy" resources alongside concealed actual supplies
- Evidence of previous "depletion" of resources
- Controlled information release suggesting different occupancy or resource profile
- Pattern disruption to prevent predictability

I once consulted with an elderly widow during a lengthy infrastructure failure who successfully deterred multiple potential intrusions through psychological deterrence alone. By creating the impression of a multi-person household with adult male members, varying light patterns to suggest group activity, and strategically playing recorded conversations, she convinced potential threats that her location presented a high-difficulty, low-reward target despite her actual vulnerability.

Security Protocols for Urban, Suburban, and Rural Settings

Security requirements vary dramatically based on population density, physical environment, and community dynamics. Adapting your approach to your specific context maximizes effectiveness while optimizing resource allocation.

Urban Environment Security Framework

High-density environments create unique security challenges requiring specific protocols:

Apartment/Condo Security Focus:

- Entry point hardening as absolute priority
- Relationship development with immediate neighbors for mutual awareness
- Sound discipline to prevent resource disclosure
- Alternative exit strategy development
- Waste management security to prevent resource indicators

Urban Single-Family Home Protocols:

- Perimeter definition using psychological boundaries
- External visual deterrents suggesting higher security than actually present
- Gray man approach to resource management
- Community integration for expanded awareness network
- Multiple-layer defensive zones from property line to safe room

Urban Movement Security:

- Irregular schedule patterns to prevent targeting
- Route variation and randomization
- Buddy system implementation whenever possible
- Gray man appearance and behavior during necessary movement
- Pre-selection of hardened locations along regular routes

During urban power outages, I documented clear outcome differences between those who implemented comprehensive security protocols and those relying solely on physical security measures. The most successful urban approach involved creating the perception of community awareness and mutual defense arrangements, effectively expanding the security perimeter beyond individual dwellings to encompass informal neighborhood watch networks.

Suburban Security Implementation

Intermediate density environments require balanced approaches leveraging both urban and rural strategies:

Perimeter Control Emphasis:

- Property boundary definition and monitoring
- Landscaping adjustments to eliminate concealment opportunities
- Access funneling to create predictable approach paths
- Neighborhood coordination for expanded awareness
- Early warning system implementation at property boundaries

Resource Visibility Management:

- Careful garden/food production concealment or disguise
- Waste management protocols to prevent supply indicators
- Activity scheduling to minimize external observation
- Delivery and supply transfer security
- Gray infrastructure (appearing less prepared than reality)

Collective Security Development:

- Neighborhood watch enhancement with communication protocols
- Mutual aid agreements with trusted neighbors
- Coordinated observation scheduling
- Information sharing systems for threat pattern identification
- Unified response protocols for specific scenarios

During hurricane recovery operations, dramatic security outcome differences between suburban neighborhoods were based almost entirely on their pre-crisis community cohesion. Areas with established neighborhood relationships and communication systems experienced minimal security incidents, while physically similar neighborhoods without these connections suffered significant property crime. The security value of known, trusted neighbors cannot be overstated in suburban environments.

Rural Security Frameworks

Low-density environments present distinct challenges requiring specialized approaches:

Approach Detection Systems:

- Early warning systems at property access points
- Driveway alarms (commercial or improvised)
- Natural channeling of approach routes for easier monitoring
- Elevated observation points for extended visibility
- Animal reaction monitoring (dogs, livestock behavior changes)

Layered Defense Implementation:

- Property boundary as initial alert perimeter
- Outbuilding security to prevent resource theft
- Primary structure hardening as final defensive position
- Distance exploitation for progressive engagement
- Concealment of high-value resources in secondary locations

Isolation Countermeasures:

- Communication redundancy (multiple systems)
- Mutual aid arrangements with distant neighbors
- Signal systems for emergency notification
- Supply cache distribution to prevent total resource loss
- Transportation security for necessary movements

During extended winter emergencies, I've worked with rural communities implementing coordinated security protocols spanning properties located miles apart. Their most effective measures focused on approach identification and communication—using pre-arranged signals (particular patterns of lights, sounds, or physical indicators) to communicate threat information across distances too great for direct communication, essentially creating a rural early warning network.

Ethical Considerations in Crisis Defense

The moral dimensions of security don't disappear during emergencies—they become more critical as social constraints weaken. Understanding ethical boundaries before crises occur prevents decision paralysis during actual threats.

The Ethical Response Continuum

Security responses exist on a continuum that should be carefully calibrated to threat level:

Avoidance: The preferred response to all potential threats

- Threat detection without engagement
- Route and pattern adjustment to prevent contact
- Profile reduction to minimize targeting
- Resource concealment to reduce motivation

Deterrence: The primary response when avoidance fails

- Clear indication of awareness and preparedness
- Verbal boundary setting with confidence
- Defensive posture establishment
- Community presence activation when available

Defense: The escalated response when deterrence fails

- Maintenance of distance from threat
- Use of barriers and obstacles
- Minimal force application necessary to neutralize threat
- Disengagement at earliest opportunity

I've interviewed dozens of crisis survivors about security incidents, and a consistent pattern emerges: those who established clear ethical boundaries before crises occurred made more effective decisions during actual threats. The time to determine your defensive ethics is now, not during an adrenaline-flooded confrontation.

Proportional Response Framework

Understanding appropriate force levels prevents both under-response and excessive reaction:

Presence Intrusion: (Trespassing without direct threat)

- Verbal notification and boundary setting
- Clear communication of awareness
- Community presence activation
- Documentation when possible

Property Threat: (Attempted theft/property damage)

- Verbal intervention from position of advantage
- Distance maintenance tools deployment
- Barrier implementation between threat and property
- Withdrawal to defensive position if resistance encountered

Physical Threat: (Danger to persons)

- Immediate movement to defensive position
- Maximum distance creation
- Defensive tool deployment as necessary
- Decisive action to neutralize immediate threat

During post-disaster recovery operations, individuals who maintained proportional response protocols experienced fewer escalated confrontations than those implementing either passive or excessively aggressive approaches. Appropriate initial response often prevents the need for higher force levels by clearly communicating both capability and restraint.

Legal Considerations Even in Crisis

Legal frameworks may change during emergencies, but they rarely disappear entirely:

Documentation Practices:

- Maintain incident log with dates, times, and specific observations
- Preserve evidence of threats when possible
- Record defensive actions taken and their results
- Document witnesses and any authority notifications

Force Justification Standards:

- Understand that legal scrutiny often follows crisis resolution
- Apply reasonable person standard to all security decisions
- Consider how actions would be perceived by uninvolved observers
- Maintain focus on threat neutralization rather than retribution

Post-Incident Protocols:

- Report significant security incidents when authorities be-

come available
- Preserve evidence of necessity and proportionality
- Document injuries and property damage
- Maintain consistent narrative based on factual events

During law enforcement absences following natural disasters, I've documented numerous cases where individuals faced legal consequences for security actions taken during the crisis period. The most defensible positions consistently involved clear necessity, proportional response, and absence of opportunity for safe withdrawal. Remember: temporary absence of law enforcement does not equate to absence of law.

Threat Assessment and Response Protocol

When facing potential security threats, this systematic assessment and response framework provides a structured approach that maximizes safety while minimizing unnecessary confrontation.

INITIAL THREAT ASSESSMENT

Is there immediate physical danger?

- **YES** → Implement immediate defensive actions
- Move to predetermined defensive position
- Create maximum distance/barriers
- Alert all household members
- Deploy defensive tools as necessary
- **NO** → Continue assessment

What is the nature of the potential threat?

- Unknown persons observing your location

- Note description, behaviors, duration
- Increase visible awareness indicators
- Alert household to potential surveillance
- Implement gray man protocols
- Unknown persons approaching your location
- Determine if approach appears purposeful or incidental
- Establish clear boundaries through presence and verbal communication
- Position for advantage while maintaining distance
- Prepare for rapid withdrawal to defensive position
- Known persons exhibiting concerning behavior
- Assess specific behavioral changes and context
- Review previous interactions for pattern establishment
- Consider resource desperation as potential motivation
- Implement appropriate boundary-setting

How many potential threats are present?

- Single individual: Maintain situational advantage through positioning
- Multiple individuals: Prioritize distance and barriers over confrontation
- Organized group: Immediate withdrawal to defensive position

CRISIS SECURITY RESPONSE QUICK START

UNCERTAIN INTENT
DO THIS:
☐ **Increase awareness**

☐ Show security presence
☐ Establish clear boundaries
☐ Activate community support

DON'T DO THIS:
☐ Directly confront
☐ Isolate yourself
☐ Show obvious preparations
☐ Use threatening language

PROPERTY THREAT
DO THIS:
☐ Set verbal boundaries
☐ Maintain physical presence
☐ Deploy distance tools
☐ Establish barriers

DON'T DO THIS:
☐ Engage physically
☐ Pursue if threat leaves
☐ Display excessive force
☐ Prioritize property over safety

PERSONAL THREAT
DO THIS:
☐ Move to safe room immediately
☐ Deploy maximum barriers
☐ Prepare defensive tools
☐ Take decisive defensive action

DON'T DO THIS:

☐ **Hesitate to respond**
☐ **Negotiate during active threat**
☐ **Fire warning shots**
☐ **Pursue beyond necessity**

Remember: *The goal is to prevent confrontation, not win it.*

COMMUNICATION PROTOCOLS

Within Household/Group:

- Establish alert signals for different threat levels
- Create clear, concise response instructions
- Assign specific roles and responsibilities
- Practice responses to ensure coordination

With Potential Threats:

- Use clear, direct language
- Establish boundaries with confidence
- Avoid threats or provocative language
- Communicate capability without escalation

With Community/Neighbors:

- Develop alert systems for mutual notification
- Create response coordination plans
- Establish regular communication schedules
- Share threat pattern information

POST-INCIDENT ACTIONS

Immediate Follow-up:

- Ensure all persons are accounted for and assessed
- Document incident details while memory is fresh
- Reinforce or repair security measures
- Implement lesson-learned improvements

Extended Response:

- Adjust patterns to prevent similar incidents
- Share relevant threat information with trusted community
- Review security protocols for potential improvements
- Address psychological impacts on household members

The goal of crisis security is not winning confrontations but preventing them entirely. Your successful security strategy is measured by the incidents that never occur because potential threats perceived your position as too difficult to target successfully. The prepared individual isn't the one with the most impressive defensive tools—it's the one who rarely needs to use them because their security posture prevents targeting in the first place.

The ultimate security paradox: those most capable of defending themselves typically face the fewest situations requiring defense.

8

When You Need to Move

There comes a moment in some crisis scenarios when staying put becomes more dangerous than leaving. In two decades of disaster response work, I've witnessed this decision point repeatedly—the reluctant acknowledgment that "bugging in" is no longer viable, followed by the chaotic scramble to evacuate without adequate preparation. The results are predictably grim.

I stood on an interstate outside New Orleans as Hurricane Katrina approached, watching families who had delayed evacuation until the last possible moment sit in gridlocked traffic as their gas gauges approached empty. I've interviewed refugees who fled urban unrest with random items thrown into garbage bags while leaving essential medications and documents behind. I've documented the aftermath of wildfire evacuations where improperly secured vehicles shed critical supplies across highways, leaving their owners without resources upon reaching safety.

The common denominator in these scenarios wasn't a lack of warning—it was the psychological barrier to making the evacuation decision, followed by the frantic, disorganized implementation once that barrier finally broke. This pattern repeats across disasters with remarkable consistency: people wait too long, then move too hastily, making critical errors that compromise their safety and survival prospects.

This chapter isn't about convincing you to evacuate—that decision depends entirely on your specific situation. It's about ensuring that if evacuation becomes necessary, you can execute it with methodical efficiency rather than panicked improvisation. We'll focus on rapid vehicle preparation, essential evacuation supplies, strategic route planning, alternative transportation options, and maintaining group cohesion during movement— all implemented with the limited time and resources available in a genuine emergency.

An evacuation executed 24 hours too early might seem unnecessary in hindsight. An evacuation executed 2 hours too late often becomes impossible to complete at all.

Vehicle Preparation in Minimal Time

Your vehicle may be your most valuable survival tool during evacuation—a potential shelter, supply carrier, and transportation system in one package. Preparing it properly, even under severe time constraints, dramatically improves your evacuation prospects.

Mechanical Readiness: The Critical First Steps

These checks require minimal time but prevent catastrophic failures during evacuation:

Fluid Level Assessment:

- Check engine oil level and condition (dark oil indicates need for change)
- Verify coolant level in reservoir (never open hot radiator cap)

- Confirm brake fluid level (low level may indicate dangerous wear)
- Check transmission fluid if accessible (typically requires engine running)
- Verify windshield washer fluid (critical for maintaining visibility)

Tire Evaluation:

- Visually inspect all tires for damage, bulges, or embedded objects
- Check pressure in all tires including spare (look for placard in driver's door jamb for correct PSI)
- Verify spare tire accessibility and proper inflation
- Confirm jack and tire changing tools are present and functional
- Tighten all visible lug nuts by hand to ensure proper seating

Battery and Electrical Quick-Check:

- Inspect battery terminals for corrosion (white/green powdery substance)
- Clean terminals with baking soda/water paste if needed
- Test headlights, brake lights, and turn signals
- Verify windshield wipers function properly
- Check that all dashboard warning lights extinguish after startup

During evacuation from advancing wildfires in California, I assisted a family whose vehicle began severely overheating after just 20 miles. A 30-second coolant check before departure would have revealed the completely empty reservoir that led to their breakdown in a high-danger zone. Their evacuation succeeded only because other evacuees sacrificed precious space to transport them. Don't become someone else's burden.

Fuel and Range Optimization

Fuel becomes a precious commodity during mass evacuations. Maximize your effective range:

Immediate Fuel Strategy:

- Fill fuel tank completely at first opportunity
- Add fuel stabilizer if available (prevents degradation during extended storage)
- Fill all approved fuel containers if time and supplies permit
- Record precise mileage and fuel level to calculate actual range
- Consider topping off even "nearly full" tanks—every gallon matters

Consumption Reduction Techniques:

- Remove unnecessary weight (100 pounds reduces efficiency by 1-2%)
- Ensure proper tire inflation (underinflation dramatically increases consumption)
- Plan routes minimizing stop/start driving and hill climbing
- Maintain steady 55-60 mph when possible (optimal efficiency for most vehicles)
- Disable unnecessary electrical systems (A/C, heated seats, etc.)

Range Extension Options:

- Calculate actual range based on 80% of fuel capacity for safety margin
- Identify potential refueling points along multiple routes
- Consider alternative routes with lower fuel requirements even if longer in distance
- Prepare jerry cans or approved containers for auxiliary fuel when appropriate
- Research alternative fuel sources for your specific vehicle (determines container requirements)

During hurricane evacuation operations, numerous families have become stranded because they began evacuation with partial tanks, assuming they could refuel along the way. Within hours, stations along major evacuation routes ran dry, stranding these partial-tank evacuees between destinations. Those who began with full tanks and additional containers maintained control of their evacuation timing and destinations.

Cargo Configuration and Vehicle Optimization

How you pack can be as important as what you pack during urgent evacuations:

Loading Priority System:

- Essential survival items accessible without complete un-loading
- Heavy items positioned low and centered over axles
- Soft items can serve as padding between hard/fragile items
- Nothing loose that could become a projectile during accident
- Critical documents and medications in passenger compart-

ment, never trunk or cargo area

Vehicle-Specific Considerations:

- Sedan: Maintain rear window visibility; utilize trunk first, then floor spaces
- SUV/Hatchback: Create tiered loading with heavy items bottom, light top
- Truck: Secure all items against wind force at highway speeds
- RV/Camper: Distribute weight evenly; prevent cabinet opening during transit
- Any vehicle: Ensure driver line of sight remains completely unobstructed

Exterior Carrying Options:

- Roof racks: Limit to lightweight, low-value items; secure thoroughly
- Trailer hitches: Verify weight rating before loading
- Bike racks: Ensure compatibility with loaded bikes
- Cargo carriers: Test latching mechanisms before departure
- All external loads: Check security at each stop; expect loosening during travel

During tornado evacuation, I assisted a family whose hastily packed SUV discharged nearly half its contents during a sharp turn, scattering irreplaceable items across a highway. The core issue wasn't the quantity they packed but the haphazard configuration that failed to account for vehicle dynamics during emergency maneuvering. Proper loading takes minutes; replacing scattered supplies may be impossible during crisis conditions.

Essential Items for Your Evacuation Kit

An effective evacuation kit balances immediate needs with longer-term utility, all within strict space and weight constraints. When every cubic inch matters, strategic selection becomes critical.

The Core Evacuation Priority Categories

Focus your limited preparation time on these essential categories:

Survival Fundamentals:

- Water: 1 gallon per person per day, minimum 3-day supply
- Nutrition: Calorie-dense, ready-to-eat foods requiring no preparation
- Shelter: Weather-appropriate clothing, emergency blankets, compact tent/tarp
- First aid: Personalized kit addressing specific family medical needs
- Medications: Minimum 7-day supply of all prescription medications

Documentation Package:

- Identity: Government-issued ID, passport, birth certificates
- Financial: Cash (small denominations), limited credit cards, bank information
- Property: Insurance policies, property deeds, vehicle titles
- Medical: Immunization records, prescriptions, medical histories
- Contact: Physical list of essential contacts with multiple

contact methods

Communication and Navigation:

- Multi-band radio (weather, AM/FM, shortwave if available)
- Mobile devices and chargers (wall, car, and ideally solar)
- Physical maps of regional and evacuation areas
- Compass and knowledge of its basic use
- Signal devices (whistle, mirror, bright fabric for daytime, light for night)

During refugee relocation work, I encountered a family who had evacuated with adequate food and water but no documentation. Their inability to prove identity or residency prevented them from accessing assistance programs, temporary housing, or banking services. "Your papers are your passport to services" became a mantra I've repeated in every evacuation planning session since.

Space-Efficient Packing Methods
Maximize limited vehicle space with these techniques:

Container Selection Strategy:

- Standardized container sizes that stack efficiently
- Rigid containers for fragile or crush-sensitive items
- Flexible containers (duffel bags, stuff sacks) for clothing and adaptable items
- Vacuum-seal bags for dramatically reducing clothing volume
- Clear containers or detailed labels for rapid content identification

Nesting and Consolidation Techniques:

- Store items inside hollow spaces of larger items
- Remove commercial packaging to reduce volume
- Consolidate multiple partial containers of same/similar items
- Roll clothing rather than folding
- Use clothing as padding between fragile items

Vehicle-Optimized Packing:

- Create "zones" within vehicle—immediate needs, secondary needs, tertiary
- Pack in reverse order of priority (items needed last loaded first)
- Utilize vertical space with appropriate securing
- Create inventory map of vehicle contents
- Ensure high-priority items remain accessible without unpacking

During flash flood evacuations, families survived when they implemented "go zone" organization systems in their vehicles—critical supplies in the passenger compartment, secondary supplies in easily accessible areas, and longer-term supplies in deeper storage. This approach allowed them to rapidly access specific supplies without unpacking their entire vehicle, a crucial advantage when operating from evacuation shelters or temporary accommodations.

The "No Regrets" Kit: When You Have Just Minutes

When evacuation time drops to minutes rather than hours, focus on these irreplaceable priorities:

Absolute Evacuation Priorities:

- People and pets above all else
- Medications (prescription and critical over-the-counter)
- Essential medical devices (mobility aids, breathing support, etc.)
- Documentation package (ID, insurance, contacts)
- Communication devices and chargers
- Vehicle keys and wallet/purse

Secondary Rapid Evacuation Items:

- Water bottle for each person
- Shelf-stable, ready-to-eat food
- Change of clothes appropriate for current weather
- Basic hygiene supplies
- Comfort items for children/vulnerable individuals
- Essential tools (multi-tool, flashlight, emergency radio)

"Grab Bag" Implementation:

- Pre-packed backpack for each household member
- Standardized core contents plus personalized essentials
- Regularly updated documentation package
- Positioned near primary exit for immediate access
- Regularly reviewed and updated to reflect changing needs

During volcanic evacuation operations, families escaped with literally two minutes' warning. Those who maintained prepared "grab bags" departed with their essential medications, documents, and basic supplies. Those without such preparation left with only the clothes they wore. The preparation time difference was minimal—less than 30 minutes to assemble basic evacuation kits—but the outcome difference was profound.

Route Planning When Everyone Is Leaving

During mass evacuations, standard navigation apps and typical route planning become dangerously unreliable. Understanding evacuation-specific navigation principles can mean the difference between successful relocation and being stranded in dangerous conditions.

Strategic Route Selection Principles

Apply these criteria when selecting evacuation routes:

Multi-Option Planning:

- Identify minimum three alternative routes from your location
- Include at least one non-obvious or secondary route
- Consider routes in opposite directions to account for threat direction changes
- Pre-calculate approximate fuel requirements for each route
- Identify critical decision points where routes diverge

Vulnerability Assessment:

- Identify potential choke points (bridges, tunnels, mountain passes)
- Note sections vulnerable to specific threats (flooding, fire, landslides)
- Locate potential alternative connections between primary routes
- Assess fuel/resource availability along each route

- Consider seasonal factors that might affect viability

Contra-Flow Consideration:

- Research historical evacuation patterns for your region
- Identify routes likely to become official evacuation corridors
- Note potential contra-flow implementation (both lanes outbound)
- Understand that official evacuation routes often experience earliest congestion
- Consider perpendicular departure from congestion flow before joining primary evacuation routes

During hurricane evacuation management, families who selected major highways as their primary evacuation routes frequently became stranded in traffic gridlock, while those who utilized secondary roads for the first 50-100 miles before connecting to major routes maintained mobility and completed evacuations successfully. The critical factor wasn't distance but maintaining movement, particularly in the initial evacuation phase.

Real-Time Route Adaptation

Dynamic response to changing conditions often proves more valuable than perfect initial planning:

Information Gathering Protocol:

- Monitor emergency broadcasts continuously
- Establish check-in points with contacts outside evacuation zone
- Observe traffic patterns personally rather than relying solely

on reports
- Triangulate information from multiple sources before major routing decisions
- Trust reports of impassable conditions but verify reports of clear routes

Adaptation Triggers:

- Define specific conditions that warrant route changes
- Establish maximum acceptable delay thresholds
- Create decision tree for common contingencies
- Pre-identify potential overnight safety locations along routes
- Determine no-go indicators that require immediate alternative action

Navigation Redundancy:

- Physical maps as primary navigation tool
- GPS devices/apps as secondary support
- Compass and landmark navigation as tertiary backup
- Written directions for critical segments
- Local knowledge gathering from other evacuees

During wildfire evacuations in the western United States, I documented multiple cases where families following static evacuation plans became trapped when fire behavior changed unexpectedly. Conversely, those implementing systematic information gathering and defined adaptation triggers successfully modified their routes in response to rapidly changing conditions, often completing evacuation despite original routes becoming compromised.

Convoy Operations and Group Movement

When traveling with multiple vehicles or families, specific protocols enhance success rates:

Convoy Configuration:

- Position most reliable vehicle in lead position
- Place vehicle with best communication capability in final position
- Keep most vulnerable individuals in middle vehicles
- Maintain visual contact between adjacent vehicles
- Establish vehicle order based on performance capabilities

Communication Systems:

- Establish primary and backup communication methods
- Create standardized signals for common situations
- Implement regular check-in protocol at predetermined intervals
- Pre-establish rally points if separation occurs
- Develop simple codes for sensitive information

Movement Discipline:

- Maintain consistent, conservative speed
- Preserve shorter following distances than normal but still safe
- Perform group stops rather than individual stops when possible
- Implement "leap-frog" fueling to maintain some vehicles

in motion
· Rotate driving responsibilities to manage fatigue

During earthquake evacuation operations, I worked with extended families evacuating as multi-vehicle groups. Those who implemented formal convoy protocols completed evacuation with all vehicles and family members intact, while those using informal "follow me" approaches frequently became separated at critical junctures, resulting in significant stress and occasional failure to reach designated safe areas.

Alternative Transportation When Vehicles Aren't Viable

When conventional vehicles become unusable due to fuel shortages, mechanical failure, or route conditions, alternative transportation methods become essential. Understanding these options before they're needed allows rapid implementation when time is critical.

Human-Powered Transportation Options

These methods require no fuel but have specific limitations and considerations:

Foot Movement Optimization:

· Maximum sustainable distance: 10-15 miles/day for average adults
· Load-carrying capacity: 15-20% of body weight for optimal endurance
· Critical equipment: Appropriate footwear, blister prevention, load-bearing systems
· Route selection criteria: Cover, concealment, gradient management
· Tactical considerations: Increased vulnerability, strict re-

source limitations

Bicycle Use:

- Maximum sustainable distance: 30-50 miles/day for average adults
- Load-carrying capacity: 30-40 pounds with proper panniers/trailers
- Critical equipment: Spare tubes, portable pump, basic tools, security devices
- Route selection criteria: Surface quality, gradient, vehicle traffic
- Tactical considerations: Increased speed and range, but higher visibility

Improvised Cart Systems:

- Construction from wheelchair components, wagons, strollers, or shopping carts
- Load capacity varies widely but typically 100-200 pounds
- Critical factors: Wheel quality, bearing maintenance, balance point
- Best practices: Test under load before relying on in emergency
- Tactical considerations: Dramatically increases carrying capacity but reduces maneuverability

During urban evacuation scenarios, there are documented remarkable success rates for bicycle evacuations compared to both vehicle and foot movement. Bicyclists' ability to bypass gridlocked traffic, find alternative pathways, and maintain 3-4 times the speed of foot travel while carrying significant supplies makes bicycles perhaps the most underrated evacuation tool, particularly for urban and suburban environments within 50 miles of safety.

Adaptive Vehicle Utilization

When conventional usage becomes impossible, vehicles can serve in alternative capacities:

Vehicle Conversion to Resource Cache:

- Immobile vehicles can serve as semi-secure storage points
- Shelter function during adverse weather
- Elevated observation platform in compatible terrain
- Signal platform using horn, lights, or reflective surfaces
- Parts harvesting for other uses (mirrors, seats, electrical components)

Alternative Fuel Adaptations:

- Wood gas conversion for compatible vehicles (advanced preparation required)
- Alcohol fuel utilization in limited applications
- Vegetable oil conversion for diesel engines
- Solar electric charging for hybrid vehicles
- Tow-starting methods for functional but battery-depleted vehicles

Improvised Vehicle Alternatives:

- Golf carts with extended battery systems
- Riding lawnmowers with cargo adaptations

- ATVs and UTVs with fuel efficiency modifications
- Motorized scooters with extended range capabilities
- Electric bicycles with solar recharging systems

During flood evacuation operations, families successfully adapted recreational vehicles (golf carts, ATVs) into primary evacuation transport when conventional vehicles became unusable due to water-covered roads. Their lower weight, adaptable route options, and modest fuel requirements allowed successful evacuation across terrain that had become impassable to standard vehicles.

Opportunity-Based Transportation

When neither personal vehicles nor human-powered options are viable, these alternatives may become available:

Evacuation Transportation Systems:

- Government-organized evacuation transport
- Non-governmental organization (NGO) evacuation assistance
- Faith-based organization transportation networks
- Commercial transportation repurposed for evacuation
- Shared transportation with other evacuees

Access Strategies:

- Pre-registration with vulnerable population registries
- Early arrival at designated pickup points
- Clear identification of special needs
- Documentation of residence within evacuation zones
- Volunteer assistance with evacuation operations

Alternative Commercial Options:

- Rental vehicles from less-affected areas
- Rideshare and taxi services (while still operating)
- Commercial bus services to evacuation destinations
- Train services if still operational
- Ferry and water transportation in compatible areas

During hurricane evacuation management, families successfully used government-organized transportation when their personal vehicles were rendered unusable. Those who registered early with evacuation assistance programs and arrived at pickup points during initial operations were consistently evacuated successfully, while those attempting to access such services after conditions deteriorated frequently found limited options.

Signals and Communication for Separated Groups

Despite best efforts, group separation during evacuation is a common reality. Establishing robust protocols for communication and reunification significantly reduces both practical and psychological impacts of temporary separation.

Communication Redundancy Planning

Build layered communication capabilities to withstand infrastructure failures:

Technology Tiers:

- Primary: Cellular phones with text capability
- Secondary: Two-way radios (FRS/GMRS) with pre-established channels
- Tertiary: Predetermined check-in protocols with out-of-area contacts

- Quaternary: Physical message systems at predetermined locations
- Final: Visual signaling systems interpretable by group members

Message Optimization:

- Develop shorthand systems for common communications
- Establish authentication methods to verify identity
- Create prioritization protocol for limited communication opportunities
- Pre-draft critical messages to minimize composition time
- Implement regular status update expectations

Communication Discipline:

- Conserve battery and operation time for essential communications
- Establish clear communication windows to preserve resources
- Implement one-way communication protocols when appropriate
- Create fallback communication schedules if primary timing fails
- Develop escalation procedures for non-response situations

During tornado evacuation operations, there is documented effectiveness of families who established out-of-area contacts as communication hubs. When local communication infrastructure failed, these distant contacts—unaffected by the regional disaster—served as information clearinghouses, relaying messages between separated family members and providing crucial coordination when direct communication became impossible.

Physical Signaling Systems

When technology-based communication fails, these systems maintain group connectivity:

Visual Signal Methods:

- Colored markers indicating movement direction and timing
- Pre-established symbols with specific meanings
- Reflective materials for nighttime visibility
- Trail marking systems using consistent indicators
- Vehicle identification through unique visual markers

Message Drop Locations:

- Predetermined sites known to all group members
- Weather-protected message containers
- Authentication methods to verify legitimate messages
- Regular check schedules aligned with group movement patterns
- Backup locations if primary sites become inaccessible

Environmental Signaling:

- Stone or stick arrangements with pre-established meanings
- Natural material patterns unlikely to occur naturally
- Modified infrastructure (tie ribbons, chalk marks, etc.)
- Night-visible indicators using reflective materials
- Sign placement considering both visibility and discretion

needs

During wildfire evacuation management, I observed families using remarkably effective low-tech communication systems—colored ribbons tied to roadside posts indicating direction of travel, safety status, and approximate timing. These simple signals allowed separated group members to successfully reconnect despite complete communication infrastructure failure in the affected region.

Reunification Protocols

Predetermined systems for reestablishing physical contact after separation:

Primary Reunification System:

- Designated meeting points in sequential priority order
- Specific timing windows for each location
- Actions to take if location becomes compromised
- Duration to remain at each point before proceeding to next
- Visual indicators of presence to leave if departing before others arrive

Rally Point Characteristics:

- Easily identifiable even under stress
- Multiple access routes
- Reasonable safety from primary threat
- Sufficient capacity for entire group
- Limited confusion with similar locations

Staged Reunification Planning:

- Initial rally points close to separation location
- Secondary points along likely evacuation routes
- Final destination reunification protocols
- Time-based progression through points
- Contingency planning for compromised locations

During earthquake response operations, I worked with several families implementing staged reunification systems. Those with clearly defined, practiced protocols successfully reconnected within 24-48 hours despite widespread infrastructure damage and communication failures. The critical success factor wasn't the specific locations chosen but the shared understanding of the sequence, timing, and alternatives if primary plans became unworkable.

The 30-Minute Evacuation Countdown

When evacuation becomes necessary with minimal warning, this structured approach maximizes both efficiency and effectiveness. Follow this sequence precisely to transform chaos into methodical action.

0-5 MINUTES: IMMEDIATE ACTIONS

Activation and Notification:

- Alert all household members using predetermined signal
- Communicate evacuation time frame clearly to all
- Make single critical external notification if applicable
- Activate any neighborhood mutual assistance agreements
- Begin evacuation countdown timer if possible

Rapid Task Assignment:

- Assign specific responsibilities to each capable household member
- Implement buddy system for vulnerable individuals
- Confirm completion expectations and accountability system
- Activate pre-planned task sequence for each person
- Establish single decision-maker for conflicting priorities

Documentation Securing:

- Retrieve pre-assembled document package
- Add any critical documents not in standard package
- Secure in waterproof, portable container
- Assign to most reliable household member
- Create duplicate set if time permits

Medication Collection:

- Gather all prescription medications
- Collect critical over-the-counter medications
- Secure in dedicated container with inventory list
- Prioritize temperature-sensitive medications for appropriate storage
- Pack administration supplies (pill cutters, measuring devices)

5-15 MINUTES: ESSENTIAL GATHERING

Survival Supply Collection:

- Deploy pre-positioned evacuation kits
- Add seasonal-specific items as needed

- Verify water supply minimum (1 gallon per person per day)
- Secure ready-to-eat food requiring no preparation
- Add critical tools based on likely evacuation conditions

Communication Preparation:

- Charge devices using vehicle adaptors during evacuation
- Pack all charging methods (wall, car, solar, battery)
- Verify functionality of non-cellular communication devices
- Distribute communication devices among multiple people
- Activate location sharing if network available

Specialized Needs Addressing:

- Child-specific supplies (diapers, formula, comfort items)
- Pet evacuation supplies (carriers, food, records)
- Medical device accessories and power supplies
- Adaptive equipment for disabled individuals
- Cultural/religious necessities for psychological well-being

Critical Resource Collection:

- Cash in small denominations
- Extra keys for all vehicles
- Weather-appropriate clothing and footwear
- Basic personal hygiene supplies
- Compact high-value items with significant utility

15-25 MINUTES: VEHICLE AND FINAL PREPARATION

Vehicle Readiness Protocol:

- Position vehicle for immediate departure
- Visually inspect tires and exterior
- Verify fuel level
- Adjust seating for evacuation configuration
- Secure any loose objects in passenger compartment

Loading Sequence Implementation:

- Load according to predefined priority system
- Position immediately needed items for accessibility
- Distribute weight appropriately
- Secure all items against movement
- Verify no loose objects in passenger compartment

Property Securing (if time permits):

- Lock all doors and windows
- Turn off utilities if appropriate for scenario
- Secure outdoor items that could become hazards
- Deploy any rapid property protection measures
- Position pre-written note for emergency services if appropriate

Final Communication Actions:

- Update out-of-area contacts with evacuation details
- Notify emergency services of evacuation if appropriate
- Mark residence as evacuated if protocol exists
- Document property condition if time permits
- Set message forwarding and out-of-office notifications

25-30 MINUTES: FINAL DEPARTURE SEQUENCE

Final Verification:

- Account for all household members
- Verify high-priority items are secured
- Confirm destination and route selection
- Review communication protocols during movement
- Establish check-in expectations and procedures

Last-Minute Additions:

- Add any overlooked critical items
- Make final decisions on borderline items
- Secure and test vehicle communications
- Verify maps and navigation tools are accessible
- Conduct final residence check if safe to do so

Departure Protocol:

- Implement predefined seating arrangement
- Test all communication devices once loaded
- Verify route accessibility before commitment
- Establish convoy procedures if multiple vehicles
- Begin movement with decisive action—hesitation costs critical time

Initial Movement Actions:

- Move decisively but drive defensively
- Implement information gathering protocol

- Maintain defined following distances if in convoy
- Begin regular check-in procedures
- Adapt immediately to observed conditions rather than assumptions

This **30-minute countdown** transforms a potentially chaotic situation into an organized, effective evacuation operation. I've implemented this exact protocol during flash flood evacuations with consistent success. The structure eliminates decision paralysis by providing clear, sequential actions that can be implemented even under extreme stress. Practice this sequence before it's needed—memory and cognition become significantly impaired during actual emergency conditions.

The goal isn't perfect evacuation; it's sufficient evacuation executed in time to matter. Don't let perfect be the enemy of survival.

9

Community and Alliance Building - Surviving Together

The lone wolf survival fantasy is perhaps the most dangerous myth in preparedness culture. I've spent decades in disaster zones, and I've never—not once—witnessed a truly solo survival success story during extended crises. The Hollywood image of the self-sufficient survivor, armed with nothing but wits and a well-stocked bunker, makes for compelling entertainment but catastrophically bad survival strategy.

Here's the reality I've documented repeatedly: in sustained emergency scenarios, individuals die, small families struggle, and communities survive. This pattern emerges with remarkable consistency whether the crisis is natural disaster, economic collapse, civil unrest, or infrastructure failure. The mathematical reality is undeniable—no individual or small family unit can maintain 24/7 security, gather all required resources, treat medical emergencies, and perform all necessary tasks while still meeting basic needs for sleep and recovery.

I've interviewed survivors who formed impromptu neighborhood security teams that successfully deterred looters when police protection evaporated. I've seen how apartment dwellers during extended urban blackouts created mutual aid networks that dramatically extended limited resources. I've observed rural communities implement cooperative labor systems during infrastructure failures that accomplished in days what would have taken individual households months to complete.

The common factor in these success stories wasn't extraordinary supplies or skills—it was the rapid formation of effective alliances. *(Survivor, the long running reality show, gets it so right that the winners form the best alliances!)* This chapter isn't about utopian community building that takes years to develop. It's about the pragmatic, sometimes uncomfortable process of quickly identifying potential allies, establishing functional resource-sharing systems, coordinating security, allocating specialized tasks, and managing the inevitable conflicts that arise under extreme stress—all within the compressed time-frame of an active crisis.

In true survival situations, the most dangerous mindset isn't paranoia or fear—it's the delusion of self-sufficiency.

Rapid Assessment of Neighbors as Potential Allies

When crisis hits, your existing neighbors—regardless of prior relationship—represent your most immediately available alliance pool. Quickly identifying who can be trusted and who should be avoided becomes a critical skill.

The Four Categories of Crisis Neighbors

Based on observed behavior patterns during actual disasters, neighbors typically fall into these categories:

The Assessed Asset: These individuals demonstrate useful skills, rational behavior, and reciprocal thinking. They contribute more than they consume within group dynamics.

- Identifying traits: Calm demeanor, practical problem-solving, resource-sharing mindset, follows through on commitments, maintains boundaries
- Typical backgrounds: Military veterans, medical professionals, tradespeople, educators, organizers
- Alliance approach: Formalize cooperative agreements quickly, establish clear mutual expectations

The Potential Asset: These individuals show mixed indicators but demonstrate core stability and potential contribution value with proper structure.

- Identifying traits: Generally cooperative but may show stress reactions, useful skills but inconsistent application, willing but sometimes unprepared
- Typical backgrounds: Office professionals, service industry workers, parents of young children
- Alliance approach: Limited initial cooperation focused on specific needs, clear boundaries, opportunity to earn increased trust

The Neutral Participant: These individuals neither significantly help nor harm group dynamics but may consume shared resources.

- Identifying traits: Minimal skill contribution, resource-limited but not demanding, follows group decisions without initiative
- Typical backgrounds: Varied, often elderly, very young, or those with limited capability
- Alliance approach: Include in peripheral support roles, mon-

itor resource consumption, provide structure and specific tasks

The Active Liability: These individuals demonstrably reduce group survival prospects through dangerous behavior, excessive resource consumption, or conflict generation.

- Identifying traits: Aggressively demanding, refuses reciprocity, creates conflict, demonstrates addictive or unstable behavior
- Typical backgrounds: Pre-crisis indicators of antisocial behavior, active addiction issues
- Alliance approach: Maintain distance, establish clear boundaries, interact only with multiple witnesses, document all interactions

During extended power outages following an ice storm, I observed a neighborhood that implemented a systematic neighbor assessment process, integrating individuals based on demonstrated behavior rather than pre-crisis social connections. They successfully incorporated several previously unknown neighbors who proved invaluable while establishing clear boundaries with others who exhibited concerning behavior. This approach prevented both naive over-inclusion and paranoid isolation— both common failure patterns in crisis communities.

Behavioral Assessment Techniques

Rather than relying on stated claims or social impressions, assess potential allies through these observable criteria:

Action-Based Evaluation:

- Observe actual behavior rather than promised behavior
- Note consistency between statements and actions
- Assess stress response patterns in challenging situations
- Evaluate resource-sharing versus resource-demanding tendencies
- Monitor boundary respect and reciprocity

Incremental Trust Building:

- Begin with small, low-risk cooperative actions
- Gradually increase scope of shared activities based on demonstrated reliability
- Implement distinct trust stages with clear criteria for advancement
- Maintain careful observation during early interactions
- Document follow-through on commitments

Risk Mitigation Strategies:

- Never expose all resources or capabilities to new alliances
- Maintain operational security regarding specialized supplies or skills
- Establish clear exit parameters for failed alliance attempts
- Keep detailed records of all resource sharing
- Always maintain fallback options for essential functions

During hurricane recovery operations, a community successfully implemented a "progressive trust" system with new members. Initial interactions involved parallel activities (working alongside but not dependent upon each other), followed by simple exchanges, then developing into interdependent activities only after reliability had been established. This methodical approach successfully integrated several valuable community members while identifying and managing individuals who proved inconsistent or disruptive.

Initial Contact and Assessment Protocol

First interactions set the tone for potential alliances. Implement this contact protocol:

Initial Approach Strategy:

- Make contact during daylight hours when possible
- Position yourself with exit path and defensive advantage
- Begin with small, specific cooperative proposal rather than general alliance
- Observe initial reaction to reasonable boundaries
- Listen more than speak during initial interaction

Information Management:

- Provide useful but non-critical information
- Avoid revealing security vulnerabilities, exact supply levels, or special capabilities
- Share general neighborhood observations without specifics
- Discuss immediate challenges rather than long-term plans
- Reciprocal information exchange should be roughly proportional

Early Warning Indicators:

- Immediate requests for significant resources
- Unwillingness to reciprocate in any capacity

- Excessive interest in your supplies, capabilities, or household composition
- Erratic emotional responses to reasonable statements
- Violation of established boundaries, even minor ones
- Evidence of substance abuse or withdrawal symptoms

I once advised a neighborhood association during an extended infrastructure failure. Their most successful alliance building began with simple, low-commitment cooperative activities— sharing information about local conditions, coordinating basic security observation, and establishing communication protocols. These initial steps required minimal trust while building the foundation for more substantive cooperation as reliability was demonstrated.

Resource Pooling Protocols and Agreements

Converting individual resource limitations into collective resource sufficiency requires structured systems rather than casual sharing. Successful crisis communities implement formal resource management even when time is limited.

Resource Inventory and Contribution Systems

Begin with systematic assessment of available resources across participating households:

Initial Resource Mapping:

- Create standardized inventory categories (water, food, medical, tools, skills)
- Implement tiered disclosure system (critical, shared, reserved)
- Document both immediate and renewable resources
- Identify unique specialist resources beneficial to community

- Quantify resource duration under various consumption scenarios

Contribution Determination:

- Establish minimum participation thresholds
- Implement proportional contribution expectations
- Account for non-material contributions (labor, skills, space)
- Create equitable valuation system for unlike resources
- Balance immediate versus sustainable contributions

Resource Documentation Protocol:

- Create written record of all pooled resources
- Implement simple but accurate tracking system
- Assign resource management responsibility
- Establish verification and audit procedures
- Create resource-specific storage and access protocols

During a prolonged winter isolation event, I worked with a rural community that worked out a formalized resource inventory system within 48 hours of the crisis onset. By documenting available supplies across 18 households, they identified critical shortages and surpluses, enabling strategic resource allocation that extended their collective sustainability by approximately 300% compared to individual household management. The critical factor wasn't the total resources but their systematic distribution and utilization.

Fair Distribution Systems

Perceived inequity rapidly destroys community cohesion.

Implement these systems to maintain fairness:

Needs-Based Allocation Framework:

- Define essential versus supplemental needs
- Account for legitimate individual differences (medical conditions, age, activity level)
- Implement transparent decision process for special requests
- Create progressive consumption restrictions as resources diminish
- Balance immediate consumption against future requirements

Contribution-Based Access System:

- Link resource access to meaningful contribution
- Account for capability differences in contribution expectations
- Implement specific accommodation for those with limited contribution capacity
- Create clear correlation between contribution and access
- Establish minimum standards applicable to all community members

Transparent Accounting Mechanisms:

- Regular resource status reports to all community members
- Clear explanation of allocation decisions
- Defined process for challenging perceived inequities
- Physical inventory verification open to member observation
- Documentation accessible to all contributing members

During flood recovery operations, a neighborhood created a simple but effective "marbles in jars" system for tracking resource contributions and allocations—using physical objects to represent resource inputs and outputs. This tangible, visible accounting system prevented the perception of favoritism that often undermines community cohesion during extended crises.

Resource Security and Access Control

Protecting pooled resources becomes a critical community function:

Physical Security Measures:

- Centralize high-value resources in defensible locations
- Implement multi-person access protocols
- Create inventory verification system during access events
- Establish resource transportation security during movement
- Develop inconspicuous storage to prevent external targeting

Operational Security Protocols:

- Need-to-know information management regarding resource locations
- Disguise resource movement and storage when possible
- Limit resource discussion to secure environments
- Create cover explanations for necessary activities
- Manage external community perception strategically

Internal Control Mechanisms:

- Dual-control access requirements for critical supplies

- Documentation of all resource movements
- Regular inventory verification procedures
- Rotation of security responsibilities among members
- Clear consequences for protocol violations

During civil unrest following an earthquake, I consulted with a community that had drawn up an effective dual-custody system for resource access—requiring two unrelated community members to be present for any significant resource distribution. This simple procedural control prevented both external theft and internal misappropriation while maintaining community trust in the fairness of the distribution system.

Security Coordination with Minimal Planning

Collective security provides exponentially better protection than individual efforts but requires structured coordination even when established under emergency conditions.

Rapid Security Framework Development

Establish these foundational security elements immediately:

Perimeter Definition and Control:

- Clearly define the protected area boundaries
- Establish observation points covering approach routes
- Implement access control procedures for entry points
- Create challenge and authentication systems
- Develop response protocols for boundary violations

Observation Shift System:

- Create sustainable rotation schedule (typically 4-hour maximum shifts)

- Pair experienced with inexperienced observers
- Implement defined observation sectors with overlap
- Establish clear reporting chain for observations
- Develop standardized alert levels and responses

Communication Protocol:

- Create simple alert signals (visual, audible, electronic)
- Establish regular check-in procedures
- Implement communication redundancy systems
- Define essential versus routine communication
- Test all systems before dependence

During extended power outages following severe storms, multiple neighborhood security systems successfully deterred opportunistic crime with minimal resources. The most effective approach involved dividing security responsibilities across multiple households, creating sustainable observation rotations that maintained 24-hour awareness without exhausting any individual members. The visibility of this coordinated presence consistently discouraged opportunistic threats.

Unified Threat Response Planning

Predefined response protocols prevent chaotic reactions to security incidents:

Threat Classification System:

- Category 1: Observation/intelligence gathering against community
- Category 2: Minor boundary testing/non-violent intrusion
- Category 3: Resource theft attempts without direct con-

frontation
- Category 4: Aggressive action against community members/resources
- Category 5: Direct violent action threatening life safety

Proportional Response Framework:

- Define appropriate responses for each threat category
- Establish clear authorization chain for response escalation
- Create multi-person verification requirement for higher responses
- Implement documentation requirements for all incidents
- Develop de-escalation procedures for all response levels

Community Mobilization Protocol:

- Establish alert signals recognizable by all members
- Define assembly points and procedures
- Create predefined responsibility assignments
- Implement accountability system during incidents
- Develop all-clear signals and verification

During hurricane recovery operations, I helped a neighborhood with a simple but effective "color code" alert system—using specific whistle patterns, visual signals, and radio codes to indicate different threat levels. This common language allowed rapid, coordinated responses to potential security concerns while minimizing confusion and preventing over-reaction to minor incidents.

Non-Confrontational Security Measures
Preventing security incidents entirely is always preferable to

successful response:

Grey Man Approach for Community:

- Minimize external visibility of resources and preparations
- Implement operational security regarding capabilities
- Create appearance of hardened target without obvious resource indicators
- Manage waste and activity visibility to prevent targeting
- Control information release to external parties

Environmental Security Design:

- Channel approach paths for maximum observation
- Create natural barriers directing movement
- Implement noise generation on likely approach routes
- Establish multiple observation points with overlapping fields
- Utilize terrain and environmental features as security multipliers

Psychological Deterrence Implementation:

- Create perception of community cohesion and awareness
- Implement visible but non-threatening presence indicators
- Establish clear boundaries through environmental cues
- Develop reputation for fairness combined with resolve
- Demonstrate capability through controlled observation

During extended civil unrest, I worked with an apartment complex that successfully prevented any significant security incidents despite surrounding areas experiencing multiple confrontations. Their approach centered on visible cooperation (regular community activities in common areas) combined with subtle security measures (overlapping observation, controlled access points, and environmental modifications that channeled all approaches through observable areas). This integrated strategy created the perception of a prepared community without presenting an aggressive security posture that might provoke confrontation.

Task Specialization in Ad-Hoc Groups

Leveraging individual capabilities through specialization dramatically increases collective effectiveness, even in rapidly formed community groups.

Capability Identification and Assignment

Systematically match tasks to capabilities rather than social position:

Skill Inventory Process:

- Create standardized skill assessment framework
- Include both certified/professional and practical skills
- Identify transferable capabilities from non-obvious backgrounds
- Document specialized knowledge from hobbies and interests
- Assess physical capabilities separately from knowledge-based skills

Role Assignment Optimization:

- Match critical functions to highest capability individuals

187

- Create redundancy in essential roles
- Consider physical limitations and age appropriateness
- Implement cross-training for critical functions
- Balance workload distribution across membership

Capability Development System:

- Identify rapid skill acquisition opportunities
- Implement apprenticeship pairings for critical skills
- Create skill-sharing sessions for general capability improvement
- Document specialized knowledge for knowledge preservation
- Develop individual improvement plans for key capabilities

During post-earthquake recovery, a community that conducted a formal "capabilities census" within 48 hours of the disaster came together. This process revealed unexpected resources—a hobby beekeeper with extensive generator maintenance knowledge, a retired teacher with wound care experience, a teenager with ham radio operations skills. By systematically matching needs to capabilities rather than making assumptions based on age, gender, or profession, they achieved significantly higher functionality than communities using arbitrary or traditional role assignments.

Functional Team Development

Organize specialized capability groups for maximum effectiveness:

Core Functional Teams:

- Security: Observation, response, perimeter management
- Resource Management: Inventory, distribution, acquisition
- Technical: Repairs, construction, systems maintenance
- Medical: First aid, preventative care, sanitation
- Logistics: Transportation, communication, coordination

Team Structure Implementation:

- Designate team leaders based on capability and temperament
- Establish clear authority boundaries for each team
- Create inter-team liaison roles for coordination
- Implement regular cross-team communication protocols
- Develop team-specific standard operating procedures

Adaptive Task Management:

- Create daily priority assessment process
- Implement task assignment and verification system
- Establish completion reporting procedures
- Develop workload balancing mechanisms
- Create flexibility for urgent requirement response

During flood recovery operations, I consulted with a community that organized into five functional teams within 72 hours of the disaster. This structure allowed parallel operations addressing different community needs simultaneously, dramatically accelerating recovery compared to centralized task management. The critical success factor was clear definition of team responsibilities combined with regular cross-team coordination meetings that maintained unity of effort.

Leadership and Coordination Structures

Effective community action requires defined decision processes:

Leadership Selection Criteria:

- Prioritize demonstrated capability over claimed authority
- Consider temperament alongside technical knowledge
- Assess communication clarity and decision quality
- Evaluate stress response patterns and consistency
- Balance decisive action with collaborative approach

Decision Authority Framework:

- Clearly define which decisions require consensus versus unilateral action
- Establish time-based decision protocols (emergency versus non-emergency)
- Create appeal process for significant decisions
- Implement documentation requirements for key decisions
- Develop review process for effectiveness assessment

Coordination Mechanism:

- Regular leadership council meetings with all team representatives
- Standardized situation reporting format
- Defined information dissemination process
- Systematic priority setting methodology
- Resource allocation arbitration process

During extended winter isolation, a rural community drafted a highly effective dual-track leadership system—a daily coordination council for routine decisions combined with clearly defined emergency decision authority. This balanced approach prevented both the paralysis of excessive consensus-seeking during urgency and the resentment caused by arbitrary unilateral decisions during normal operations.

Conflict Resolution in High-Stress Environments

Conflict inevitably emerges in crisis communities. Having structured resolution systems prevents escalation that threatens group cohesion.

Early Intervention Protocols

Address conflicts before they reach destructive levels:

Conflict Identification Indicators:

- Increasing communication avoidance between individuals
- Faction formation around specific individuals
- Resource hoarding or accounting challenges
- Compliance reduction with community standards
- Emotional escalation during routine interactions

Immediate De-escalation Techniques:

- Physical separation of involved parties
- Cooling-off period implementation
- Neutral third-party initial intervention
- Focus on immediate behavior rather than patterns
- Environmental modification to reduce stress factors

Structured Initial Resolution Approach:

- Create private discussion environment
- Implement turn-based communication format
- Focus on specific behaviors rather than character
- Identify concrete, actionable resolution steps
- Document agreements and follow-up requirements

During hurricane recovery operations, I worked with a shelter that put in place a "48-hour rule." Any observed conflict indicators triggered immediate intervention before the situation could escalate. This proactive approach successfully resolved approximately 80% of potential conflicts at the initial stage, preventing the faction-forming and group deterioration that often plagues crisis communities.

Formal Mediation System

When initial intervention proves insufficient, implement structured mediation:

Mediation Team Structure:

- Select mediators based on perceived neutrality and temperament
- Create balanced team representing different community segments
- Establish clear mediator authority limitations
- Implement recusal procedures for conflicts of interest
- Develop decision recording and implementation monitoring

Mediation Process Implementation:

- Private individual interviews before joint session
- Structured presentation of perspectives without interrup-

tion
- Focus on interests rather than positions
- Generate multiple solution options before evaluation
- Create concrete, measurable resolution agreements

Follow-up and Accountability:

- Schedule specific implementation verification
- Document compliance with agreements
- Implement progressive consequences for agreement violations
- Create restoration path for relationships when possible
- Establish pattern monitoring for recurring issues

During wildfire evacuation sheltering, a community instituted a remarkably effective three-person mediation team structure—one person selected by each party in conflict plus one selected by consensus. This balanced approach created the perception of fairness while ensuring all perspectives received consideration, resulting in high compliance with mediated resolutions.

Irreconcilable Conflict Management

Some conflicts can't be fully resolved in crisis conditions. Manage these situations:

Containment Strategies:

- Implement contact limitation protocols
- Create separate operational spheres when possible
- Establish neutral buffer individuals for necessary interaction
- Develop compartmentalized responsibility areas

- Implement strict interaction guidelines for required contact

Community Impact Minimization:

- Prevent faction development through individual management
- Address rumors and misinformation proactively
- Focus community attention on shared challenges
- Implement temporary structure modifications if necessary
- Create consequences for faction promotion

Last Resort Options:

- Establish community standards violation procedures
- Implement proportional, documented consequences
- Create restoration pathways when possible
- Develop separation protocols when necessary
- Establish resource division procedures for irreconcilable situations

During a civil unrest, I worked with a neighborhood association managing a situation involving two community members with fundamentally incompatible approaches to security coordination. Rather than forcing artificial resolution, they implemented a geographical responsibility division that minimized contact while maintaining overall community function. This pragmatic approach acknowledged the reality that some conflicts require management rather than resolution during active crisis conditions.

Community Resource Assessment Tool
Effective community formation requires systematic evalua-

tion of both human and material resources. This assessment framework provides the foundation for sustainable crisis communities developed under urgent conditions.

HUMAN RESOURCE ASSESSMENT

Individual Capability Inventory:

- Medical skills and experience level
- Security training and capability
- Technical knowledge (electrical, mechanical, structural)
- Food production/preservation experience
- Leadership and organizational ability
- Communication skills (including languages, radio operation)
- Psychological strengths (stress tolerance, conflict resolution)

Special Needs Identification:

- Medical conditions requiring ongoing management
- Medication dependencies
- Mobility limitations
- Dietary restrictions
- Sensory limitations (vision, hearing)
- Age-related considerations (very young, elderly)
- Psychological vulnerabilities

Contribution Capacity Assessment:

- Physical labor capability
- Technical skill application

- Knowledge transfer ability
- Decision-making capacity
- Resource contribution potential
- Time availability
- Specialized equipment availability

MATERIAL RESOURCE INVENTORY

Survival Fundamentals Assessment:

- Water: Current supply and acquisition capability
- Food: Inventory by type and shelf life
- Shelter: Structural integrity and capacity
- Medical supplies: Inventory by category
- Hygiene/sanitation resources
- Security tools and equipment
- Communication devices and capabilities

Sustainability Resources Evaluation:

- Energy generation capacity
- Food production capability
- Water collection/purification systems
- Waste management solutions
- Tool inventory and condition
- Repair parts and materials
- Education and reference resources

Specialized Equipment Inventory:

- Transportation assets

- Power generation equipment
- Food processing tools
- Construction equipment
- Communication systems
- Medical devices
- Security equipment

COMMUNITY STRUCTURE DEVELOPMENT

Leadership and Decision Process:

- Clear authority boundaries
- Decision-making methodology
- Information flow system
- Conflict resolution process
- Accountability mechanisms
- Adaptation/learning procedures
- Documentation requirements

Operational Systems Implementation:

- Regular meeting schedule and format
- Task assignment and verification process
- Resource allocation procedures
- Work scheduling methodology
- Performance evaluation mechanism
- Standardized reporting formats
- Record keeping requirements

Community Standards Establishment:

- Membership criteria and responsibilities
- Contribution expectations
- Resource sharing protocols
- Conflict management procedures
- Privacy and boundary guidelines
- Security participation requirements
- Consequences for standards violations

COMMUNITY VIABILITY ASSESSMENT

Rate each factor 1-5 (higher is better) to evaluate sustainability potential:

Resource Factors:

- Water security: _____
- Food sustainability: _____
- Shelter adequacy: _____
- Energy availability: _____
- Medical capability: _____
- Security capacity: _____
- Knowledge base: _____

Human Factors:

- Skill diversity: _____
- Leadership quality: _____
- Group cohesion: _____
- Conflict management: _____
- Adaptive capacity: _____
- Work capacity: _____

- Psychological resilience: _____

Environmental Factors:

- Location defensibility: _____
- Climate suitability: _____
- Resource accessibility: _____
- Threat exposure: _____
- Isolation/accessibility: _____
- Production capacity: _____
- Long-term habitability: _____

TOTAL SCORE: _____/105

90-105: Exceptional viability prospects **75-89**: Strong viability with minor enhancements needed **60-74**: Moderate viability requiring significant improvements **45-59**: Challenged viability requiring immediate intervention **Below 45**: Critical deficiencies threatening basic sustainability

This assessment framework provides both structure for initial community formation and a roadmap for targeted improvement. I've implemented this exact assessment model during disaster recovery operations with consistently positive results. The process itself builds community cohesion while creating the shared understanding necessary for effective cooperation under crisis conditions.

The goal isn't creating a perfect community—it's establishing a functional alliance system capable of meeting survival needs more effectively than individual efforts could achieve. Even an imperfect community typically outperforms isolated individuals or families during extended crisis scenarios.

10

Staying Informed When Systems Fail

In every disaster I've responded to, from hurricanes to civil unrest, the same desperate question emerges within hours: "What's happening?" The human need for information becomes almost as visceral as the need for water or shelter. This isn't just psychological comfort—it's survival-critical intelligence that determines your next actions.

Families make catastrophic evacuation decisions based on rumors that could've been dispelled with basic information verification. I've seen communities tear themselves apart over resource allocation when simple communication protocols could have prevented conflict. There are countless cases where individuals with functioning communication tools survived while those without them perished—not because they called for rescue, but because they received crucial information that allowed them to make life-saving decisions.

The collapse of conventional information infrastructure follows a predictable pattern: cellular networks become overloaded first, internet connectivity follows shortly after, and broadcast systems often continue functioning but with increasingly un-reliable information. This progressive degradation creates an information vacuum rapidly filled by rumor, speculation, and deliberate misinformation—all of which can prove deadly in crisis environments.

This chapter isn't about building elaborate communications systems you don't have time to acquire. It's about leveraging what's available, establishing verification protocols for the information you receive, creating resilient networks with min-imal technology, maintaining contact when technology fails entirely, and protecting your communications from intercep-tion that could compromise your security. The goal isn't perfect information—it's sufficient intelligence to make decisions that enhance rather than degrade your survival prospects.

In crisis situations, accurate information and reliable com-munication aren't luxuries—they're force multipliers that sig-nificantly increase your survival probability.

Last-Minute Communication Gear Acquisition

When disaster is imminent, strategic communication tool acquisition becomes a high-priority task. Focus on these systems based on reliability during infrastructure failure.

Radio Systems: Your Communication Backbone

Radio technology represents your most resilient communica-tion option during infrastructure collapse:

Weather Radio Priorities:

- NOAA Weather Radio with SAME technology (Specific Area Message Encoding)
- Battery operation with hand-crank backup charging
- Multiple power options (AC, battery, solar, crank)

- External antenna capability for reception improvement
- Programmable for your specific county/region alerts

Two-Way Radio Acquisition:

- Family Radio Service (FRS) radios for short-range communication (0.5-2 miles)
- General Mobile Radio Service (GMRS) radios for increased range (2-5+ miles)
- Look for units with:
- Multiple power options including rechargeable batteries
- Privacy codes (reduces interference but doesn't provide security)
- Weather alert reception capabilities
- Water resistance for all-weather use
- VOX (voice activation) for hands-free operation

AM/FM Broadcast Reception:

- Vehicle radio systems (often overlooked but highly effective)
- Portable radios with multiple power options
- Emergency crank radios with broadcast reception
- Shortwave capability for distant information sources
- Digital display for precise frequency tuning

During Hurricane Maria's aftermath, multiple isolated communities maintained situational awareness exclusively through battery-powered radio reception. While lacking cellular and internet connectivity for weeks, these communities received critical information about aid distribution, dangerous conditions, and recovery operations through broadcast radio systems that continued functioning despite massive infrastructure damage.

Power Maintenance for Communication Systems
Communication tools require power. Prioritize these options:

Battery Inventory and Acquisition:

- Standard batteries (AA, AAA, C, D) for common devices
- Specialized batteries for specific communication tools
- Lithium batteries for extended shelf life and cold-weather performance
- Alkaline batteries for general applications
- Rechargeable options with multiple charging methods

Charging System Priorities:

- Multi-device USB charging systems
- Solar chargers with battery storage
- Hand-crank emergency chargers
- Vehicle charging systems with multiple adapters
- Power bank batteries with highest capacity-to-weight ratio

Power Conservation Strategies:

- Cycle devices on specific schedule rather than continuous operation
- Establish communication windows to preserve battery life
- Remove batteries from devices when not in active use
- Maintain some devices in fully-charged standby mode
- Implement strict discipline regarding unnecessary power

use

During extended winter power outages, families maintained communication capability for weeks through systematic power management—operating devices on strict schedules, consolidating charging activities during vehicle operation, and implementing a disciplined battery rotation system. The critical factor wasn't the quantity of batteries but the systematic approach to their deployment and conservation.

Communication Documentation Tools

Often overlooked, physical documentation becomes crucial when digital systems fail:

Message Recording Systems:

- Waterproof notebooks for persistent information
- Standardized message forms for consistent information recording
- Carbon-copy or duplicate recording for message retention
- Pencils (function in all weather conditions) and pens
- Message organization system (chronological, source-based, or priority)

Information Management Tools:

- Map marking supplies for graphical information recording
- Message boards for community information sharing
- Standardized symbols for common information categories
- Location documentation system for geographic information
- Filing system for information retention and retrieval

Visual Communication Supplies:

- High-visibility marking materials
- Standardized signal symbols
- Weather-resistant marking tools
- Ground-to-air communication symbols
- Night-visible signaling options

During wildfire evacuations, families with physical information management systems maintained significantly better situational awareness than those relying entirely on electronic systems. Their ability to record broadcast information, track rapidly changing evacuation zones on physical maps, and maintain documented communication logs proved invaluable when electronic systems failed due to power loss or infrastructure damage.

Information Verification in Crisis Situations

During emergencies, information quality degrades rapidly while its importance increases exponentially. Implementing verification protocols becomes survival-critical.

The SALTS Verification Framework

Apply this systematic assessment to all critical information:

Source Assessment:

- Official sources (government, emergency management agencies)
- Firsthand observers with direct knowledge
- Trusted network members with verification capability
- News organizations with professional standards
- Anonymous or unverified sources (lowest reliability)

Age Evaluation:

- Information timestamp or origination time
- Relevance decay based on information type
- Update frequency of the information source
- Comparison with known timeline of events
- Contextual time markers within information

Location Specificity:

- Geographic precision of the information
- Relevance to your specific location
- Distance decay factor for applicability
- Terrain and infrastructure considerations
- Directional components (especially for threat movement)

Triangulation Process:

- Verification from multiple independent sources
- Consistency across different information channels
- Alignment with observable conditions
- Correlation with predictable patterns
- Resolution of conflicting information elements

Specificity Assessment:

- Detail level suggesting firsthand knowledge
- Appropriate technical precision
- Absence of vague qualifiers and generalities
- Contextual elements demonstrating familiarity
- Precision appropriate to source's expected knowledge

During hurricane response operations, communities that worked out formal information verification protocols significantly improved decision quality. By requiring multiple-source confirmation before acting on critical information and systematically evaluating information against the SALTS framework, these communities avoided the resource-wasting false alarms and dangerous missed warnings that plagued areas relying on unverified information.

Rumor Control Mechanisms

Misinformation spreads exponentially during crises. Implement these countermeasures:

Community Information Clearing Process:

- Designate specific verification responsible persons
- Implement formal information validation procedures
- Create regular information dissemination schedule
- Establish rumor reporting mechanism
- Document and correct identified misinformation

Pattern Recognition in Misinformation:

- Excessive specificity in predictions
- Information triggering strong emotional responses
- Claims of unique access or insider knowledge
- Information aligning too perfectly with hopes or fears
- Resistance to verification or source disclosure

Psychological Inoculation Against Rumors:

- Understand normal information degradation in crises

- Recognize common rumor patterns before encountering them
- Implement default skepticism for high-consequence information
- Develop patience with partial information rather than seeking completeness
- Distinguish between operational needs and information desires

During civil unrest, I consulted with neighborhood associations establishing formal rumor control systems—designating specific individuals responsible for information verification and creating regular "information updates" that addressed circulating rumors with verified facts. Communities using these systems demonstrated significantly better decision quality and resource allocation than those where information flowed without verification mechanisms.

Information Triage and Prioritization

Not all information has equal value. Implement this prioritization framework:

Critical Survival Information:

- Immediate safety threats (fire movement, flooding, civil danger)
- Essential resource availability (water, food, medical)
- Infrastructure status affecting life safety (power, water, gas)
- Evacuation requirements and routes
- Weather events affecting survival conditions

High-Value Operational Information:

- Recovery resource availability and locations
- Transportation route status
- Security situation in surrounding areas
- Disease/health threat developments
- Authority directives affecting movement or resources

Contextual Understanding Information:

- Scope and scale of the emergency
- Estimated duration of different crisis phases
- Regional conditions beyond immediate area
- Historical patterns in similar situations
- Long-term projection information

During flood response operations, I worked with communities creating information priority systems that focused limited communication resources on life-safety information first, operational information second, and contextual information third. This structured approach ensured that when communication opportunities were limited, the most survival-critical information received transmission priority.

Alternative Information Networks

When conventional information sources fail, alternative networks become essential. These systems often continue functioning when primary infrastructure collapses.

Community Intelligence Networks

Human networks often outlast technological systems during disasters:

Neighborhood Information Exchange:

- Designated information gathering/distribution points
- Regular scheduled information sharing sessions
- Standardized reporting format for consistency
- Defined verification responsibilities
- Information distribution responsibilities

Hub-and-Spoke Intelligence Systems:

- Central information consolidation point
- Designated sector information gatherers
- Regular physical information transfer schedule
- Information synthesis and analysis function
- Standardized distribution mechanism

Linear Distribution Networks:

- House-to-house information transmission
- Message verification and authentication system
- Transmission redundancy to prevent degradation
- Message prioritization protocols
- Acknowledgment and feedback mechanisms

During urban power outages, apartment buildings have cobbled together remarkably effective floor-by-floor information distribution systems—designating floor captains responsible for information gathering and distribution, with regular building-wide information consolidation meetings. This human network maintained comprehensive situational awareness despite complete technological communication failure.

Radio-Based Information Systems

Various radio services continue functioning during infrastructure collapse:

Emergency Broadcasting Monitoring:

- Emergency Alert System (EAS) through AM/FM stations
- NOAA Weather Radio continuous broadcasts
- Local government emergency radio systems
- Designated emergency information stations
- Scheduled official information broadcasts

Amateur Radio Networks:

- Local ham radio emergency networks
- Scheduled emergency nets on predetermined frequencies
- Traffic passing systems for message relay
- Weather spotting networks
- Emergency operations center communications

Non-Traditional Radio Resources:

- Business band radio systems
- Civil Air Patrol communications
- Marine band radio in coastal areas
- Public service scanning for situational awareness
- Satellite radio broadcasting (often continues when terrestrial systems fail)

During hurricane recovery operations, communities have maintained comprehensive situational awareness exclusively

211

through radio-based information systems. By establishing systematic monitoring schedules for different radio services and information sharing protocols, these communities maintained better awareness than areas with sporadic cellular/internet connectivity, as the radio information came directly from emergency management sources rather than filtered through unreliable social media channels.

Asynchronous Communication Systems

When real-time communication becomes impossible, these systems maintain information flow:

Physical Message Exchange Points:

- Community bulletin boards at central locations
- Message drop boxes with regular collection
- Standardized message forms for consistency
- Designated message clearinghouse responsibilities
- Regular message delivery/collection schedule

Unmanned Information Caches:

- Weather-protected information posting locations
- Map update stations with current hazard marking
- Resource availability notification points
- Missing persons information coordination
- Regular update schedules for time-sensitive information

Mobile Information Distribution:

- Courier systems along established routes
- Information distribution during resource delivery

- Mobile bulletin boards on vehicles
- Scheduled information broadcast at community points
- Information distribution integrated with other essential functions

During extended winter isolations, rural communities have built highly effective "mailbox information exchanges"—using existing mailbox locations as information transfer points with weather-protected message containers and regular collection schedules. This system maintained community-wide information dissemination despite impassable roads and non-existent telecommunications.

Signal Methods When Technology Fails

When all technological communication fails, traditional signaling systems become essential. These methods have functioned effectively for centuries and remain viable during complete infrastructure collapse.

Visual Signaling Systems

Visual signals provide effective communication over varying distances:

Daylight Visual Signals:

- Flag systems using color and movement patterns
- Signal mirrors for long-distance communication
- Smoke signals with pattern/timing meaning
- Symbol/sign posting at predetermined locations
- Movement/gesture systems for close-range communication

Low-Light Visual Signals:

- Flashlight/signal lamp with simple code systems
- Fire positioning and pattern systems
- Glow stick patterns and movements
- Reflective material signals
- Light/dark patterns created with barriers

Symbol-Based Communication:

- Ground-to-air emergency symbols
- Standardized hazard marking systems
- Route marking for navigation guidance
- Resource location indication
- Need category symbolization

During backcountry search operations, I've used standardized visual signal systems that successfully communicated complex information over significant distances. The key elements were pre-established signal meanings, regular observation periods, and confirmation signals acknowledging reception—principles directly applicable to disaster communication when technological systems fail.

Acoustic Signaling Methods

Sound-based signals function in conditions that defeat visual communication:

Simple Acoustic Codes:

- Whistle blast patterns (3 blasts universally indicates emergency)
- Horn or bell ringing sequences
- Vehicle horn patterns

- Improvised percussion signals
- Voice amplification techniques

Pattern-Based Acoustic Systems:

- Timing variations to convey different meanings
- Pattern repetition for emphasis or urgency
- Direction-based meaning variations
- Duration-encoded information
- Multi-source triangulation signaling

Environment-Specific Adaptations:

- Urban acoustic signal considerations
- Wilderness sound propagation techniques
- Weather impact adaptations
- Terrain utilization for sound channeling
- Background noise compensation methods

During forest firefighting operations, I've employed acoustic signal systems that maintained crew communication even when visual contact was impossible due to smoke conditions. Using simple pattern-based whistle signals with standardized meanings and acknowledgment protocols, these systems provided essential coordination capability without any technology.

Physical Message Transport

When no remote communication is possible, physical message delivery becomes essential:

Message Standardization:

- Consistent format for essential information
- Prioritization indicators for urgency
- Authentication elements to verify source
- Environmental protection for message integrity
- Multiple copies for redundancy

Route and Schedule Systems:

- Established message delivery routes
- Regular schedule expectations
- Alternative route planning for obstacles
- Schedule modification signals
- Contingency planning for route compromise

Courier Selection and Operation:

- Selection criteria for message carriers
- Essential equipment for message transport
- Security protocols for sensitive information
- Contingency instructions for various scenarios
- Authentication systems for courier verification

During extended disaster recovery operations, remarkably effective physical message networks have been created using predetermined routes, standardized message formats, and regular scheduling. These systems provided reliable communication between isolated communities when all technological options had failed, enabling coordination of resource sharing and mutual assistance that significantly improved survival outcomes.

Operational Security for Your Communications

During crises, communication security takes on critical importance as normal social constraints weaken. Protecting information integrity and controlling access becomes essential.

Threat Assessment for Communications

Understand the specific risks to different types of communication:

Physical Communication Threats:

- Message interception during physical transport
- Observation of visual signals by unintended recipients
- Bulletin board/public information compromise
- Physical eavesdropping on conversations
- Message repository tampering or monitoring

Electronic Communication Vulnerabilities:

- Radio transmission interception (all radio is intercept-able)
- Cell phone communication vulnerability
- Unencrypted digital communication exposure
- Metadata exposure revealing patterns and connections
- Device theft providing access to stored communications

Social Engineering Exploits:

- Information elicitation through casual conversation
- False identity or authority claims to access information
- Confidence exploitation to bypass security measures
- Manufactured urgency to circumvent verification
- Relationship leverage to obtain sensitive information

During civil unrest situations, groups have created communication security protocols based on specific threat assessment rather than general paranoia. By identifying which information required protection and which specific threats were likely, they developed proportional security measures that protected critical information without creating paralyzing operational friction.

Practical Communications Security Measures

Implement these measures based on specific protection requirements:

Physical Communication Security:

- Need-to-know distribution limitation
- Trusted courier utilization
- Authentication systems for message verification
- Indirect routing to mask origins/destinations
- Dead drop systems for high-security exchanges

Electronic Security Implementation:

- Frequency management for radio communications
- Code word substitution for sensitive information
- Transmission timing and duration discipline
- Power management to limit transmission range
- Antenna configuration to control signal propagation

Operations Security Integration:

- Information compartmentalization by sensitivity
- Regular communication pattern maintenance
- Deception integration when appropriate

- Regular security procedure modification
- Compromise indicators and responses

During emergency operations, I've worked with communities that instituted simple but effective communication security— using basic code word substitution for sensitive resource information, limiting detailed communications to in-person exchanges, and implementing authentication challenges for community members. These measures effectively prevented resource targeting while maintaining operational effectiveness.

Code and Authentication Systems

Simple security measures significantly enhance communication protection:

Basic Code Systems:

- Word substitution for sensitive terms
- Reference point systems for location information
- Predetermined context understanding
- Innocent phrase transformations
- Numeric code derivation from shared knowledge

Authentication Protocols:

- Challenge-response systems using pre-shared information
- Personal knowledge verification questions
- Physical token presentation requirements
- Multi-factor verification for critical communications
- Out-of-band verification for high-security needs

Communications Discipline:

- Minimizing sensitive content in vulnerable channels
- Regular procedure review and modification
- Compromise indication and response planning
- Regular security practice integration
- Accountability for security violations

During disaster response operations involving valuable resource distribution, I built a simple but effective authentication system—combining physical identification, knowledge-based challenges, and community vouching to verify legitimate communication. This multi-layered approach prevented multiple attempted deceptions while maintaining operational efficiency for legitimate communications.

Emergency Information Hierarchy

During crises, not all information carries equal importance. This prioritization framework ensures critical information receives appropriate attention while preventing information overload that degrades decision quality.

INFORMATION PRIORITY CLASSIFICATION

CATEGORY 1: IMMEDIATE LIFE SAFETY

- Imminent threat warnings (fire, flood, hazmat, violence)
- Evacuation orders and routes
- Emergency medical information
- Critical infrastructure failures affecting safety
- Extreme weather warnings with imminent impact

CATEGORY 2: URGENT OPERATIONAL NEEDS

- Resource availability information (water, food, medicine)
- Shelter status and availability
- Transportation route conditions
- Rescue and emergency service availability
- Immediate security situation updates

CATEGORY 3: CRITICAL PLANNING INFORMATION

- Extended weather forecasts affecting operations
- Disease outbreak/health threat developments
- Resource projection information
- Infrastructure restoration timelines
- Official recovery and response planning

CATEGORY 4: SITUATIONAL UNDERSTANDING

- Scope and scale of the emergency
- Conditions in surrounding areas
- Historical patterns in similar situations
- Longer-term projections and timelines
- Contextual information for decision-making

CATEGORY 5: GENERAL INFORMATION

- Non-local emergency developments
- Background information on conditions
- Historical context for current situation
- General news and non-critical updates
- Community and social information

INFORMATION SOURCE RELIABILITY RANKING

Rate sources using this reliability scale:

A-LEVEL SOURCES: MAXIMUM RELIABILITY

- Direct personal observation of the information
- Official emergency management agencies
- First responders with direct involvement
- Technical specialists within their expertise
- Instrumentation and direct measurement

B-LEVEL SOURCES: HIGH RELIABILITY

- Trusted network members with verification capability
- Official sources for non-local information
- Professional news organizations with standards
- Technical sources outside primary expertise
- Multiple consistent second-hand reports

C-LEVEL SOURCES: MODERATE RELIABILITY

- General news reports without specific sourcing
- Trusted individuals reporting second-hand information
- Official sources for information outside their jurisdiction
- Historical patterns applied to current situations
- Technical information from general sources

D-LEVEL SOURCES: LOW RELIABILITY

- Unverified social media information
- Anonymous reports without corroboration
- Rumor-based information with partial details

- Extrapolations beyond available data
- Sources with known biases or agendas

E-LEVEL SOURCES: MINIMAL RELIABILITY

- Unverified third-hand information
- Anonymous sources with dramatic claims
- Information contradicting established facts
- Sources with history of inaccuracy
- Claims requiring conspiracy or unlikely coordination

EMERGENCY INFORMATION HANDLING PROTOCOL
PRIORITY 1: LIFE SAFETY INFORMATION
Examples: Imminent threats, evacuation orders, dangerous conditions

VERIFICATION:

- Confirm with trusted official source
- Get multiple confirmations when possible
- Verify immediately

DISTRIBUTION:

- Alert everyone immediately
- Use all available communication methods
- Notify most affected areas first

UPDATES:

- Continuous updates until threat passes
- Regular status reports
- Clear "all-clear" notification

PRIORITY 2: CRITICAL RESOURCES
Examples: Water, food, medicine, shelter, transportation routes

VERIFICATION:

- Trusted source required
- Cross-check information
- Evaluate source reliability

DISTRIBUTION:

- Regular scheduled announcements
- Post at community gathering points
- Notify affected sectors

UPDATES:

- Update at scheduled times
- Immediate alerts for major changes
- Daily summary

PRIORITY 3: PLANNING INFORMATION
Examples: Weather forecasts, health trends, infrastructure timelines

VERIFICATION:

- Multiple sources preferred
- Look for consistent information
- Analyze trends

DISTRIBUTION:

- Include in daily briefings
- Post on community bulletin boards
- Share at information centers

UPDATES:

- Daily updates
- Special notices for significant changes
- Track changes over time

PRIORITY 4-5: BACKGROUND INFORMATION
Examples: Situation overview, conditions in other areas, historical context

VERIFICATION:

- Basic source assessment
- General fact-checking
- Focus on relevance

DISTRIBUTION:

- Include in situation summaries
- Make available as reference
- Low-priority distribution

UPDATES:

- Update as resources permit
- Non-time-sensitive distribution
- Consolidate with other information

REMEMBER:

- Higher priority information always takes precedence
- Document source, time, and distribution of critical information
- Clearly mark updates and changes to previously shared information
- Verify more thoroughly as consequences increase

INFORMATION VERIFICATION CHECKLIST

For critical information, verify using these questions:

☐ Has the information been confirmed by at least two independent sources?

☐ Is the information consistent with known facts and current conditions?

☐ Does the source have direct knowledge or official responsibility?

☐ Is the information specific regarding time, location, and details?

☐ Has similar information proven accurate in the past?

☐ Does the information make logical sense given the current situation?

☐ Has contradictory information been evaluated and resolved?

☐ Has the information been verified by subject matter experts when technical?

☐ Is the information appropriately detailed for the source's access level?

☐ Has the information been assessed for potential manipulation or agenda?

During disaster response operations, I've used this exact information hierarchy system with multiple communities. The structured approach prevented both the dangerous dismissal of critical information and the equally dangerous overconsumption of low-value information that often leads to decision paralysis. Communities utilizing this system maintained consistently better situational awareness and made more effective decisions than those using ad hoc information management.

In crisis situations, information management isn't about knowing everything—it's about knowing the right things at the right time to make decisions that enhance survival. This systematic approach ensures you focus limited attention on the information that matters most while maintaining the contextual understanding necessary for effective adaptation.

11

The First Week and Beyond:
Transitioning to Long-Term Survival

The ancient Romans had a saying: "Fortune favors the prepared mind." In my experience responding to disasters, I've found a corollary that's just as true: misfortune punishes the partially prepared. I've watched as families who brilliantly managed the first 72 hours of a crisis gradually unraveled during the following weeks. Their initial preparation gave them a tremendous advantage—until those preparations ran out. Then they faced the harsh reality of long-term adaptation with neither the resources nor the mindset required for sustained survival.

The one-week mark represents a critical psychological and practical threshold in any crisis. It's when the adrenaline begins to fade. When the reality of your situation truly settles in. When improvisation must transform into systems. When reaction must evolve into strategy. The difference between those who continue to thrive and those who begin to deteriorate typically isn't found in their initial preparations—it's in their ability to transition from emergency response to sustainable operation.

I remember sitting with Jorge, a 68-year-old grandfather

in Puerto Rico, three weeks after Hurricane Maria. His initial preparation had been impressive—water, food, medical supplies, even a small generator. But as we talked in the remains of his once-immaculate garden, now converted into a rudimentary vegetable plot, he shared the insight that saved his family: "The hurricane lasted a day. The emergency lasted a week. But the crisis—that is measured in seasons, not days."

This chapter isn't about perpetuating the fantasy of returning to normal. It's about the practical, sometimes uncomfortable reality of creating a new normal when the old one isn't coming back anytime soon. We'll explore how to extend your initial preparations through intelligent rationing and replenishment, how to manage the psychological challenges of extended crisis conditions, which skills provide the highest return on your limited learning time, and how to balance between preparing for eventual recovery and adapting to potentially permanent change.

The first week is about survival. Everything beyond is about living. There's a world of difference between the two.

Extending Your Emergency Preparations

The supplies you've gathered for immediate survival were never intended to last indefinitely. Extending their functional lifespan requires both practical techniques and strategic thinking.

The morning after Hurricane Katrina made landfall, I met a family who proudly showed me their emergency water supply— nearly thirty gallons stored in various containers. "That should last us at least two weeks," the father confidently stated. By my calculation, with five family members in the Louisiana August heat, they had perhaps three days if strictly rationed. Their fundamental error wasn't in the quantity they'd stored but in their consumption assumptions. This pattern repeats across nearly every resource category in extended emergencies.

Water presents your most immediate extension challenge. Most families store enough for 3-7 days based on the standard guideline of one gallon per person per day. Extending this supply begins with radical consumption honesty. Drinking requirements are non-negotiable—typically about two quarts per person daily in moderate temperatures, more in heat. But every other water use can be dramatically modified.

Institution of a "navy shower" protocol—getting wet, turning off water, soaping, then briefly rinsing—can reduce bathing consumption by 90%. Implementing wash basin bathing instead of showers reduces it further. Cooking methods can be adapted to minimize water usage—one-pot meals rather than multiple components, selecting foods that absorb cooking water rather than require draining, reusing cooking water for multiple purposes.

The most successful water extension strategy I've witnessed came from an elderly couple in the aftermath of a major earthquake. They established a strict water use progression: drinking water became cooking water, cooking water became washing water, washing water became toilet flushing water. Nothing was used only once. Through this system, they maintained hygiene and hydration for nearly three weeks on supplies intended for one.

Food supplies present different extension challenges. The natural impulse during stress is to overconsume—both from psychological comfort seeking and the increased caloric demands of crisis activity. Countering this requires structured consumption protocols. Institute fixed meal times rather than grazing. Prepare precise portions rather than self-service.

Create explicit caloric allocations based on activity levels and physical requirements.

The most effective food extension strategy balances caloric maintenance with psychological satisfaction. During an extended urban crisis, I observed a family implement a brilliant rotation system—alternating their limited "comfort foods" with their bulk staples rather than consuming all the preferred items first. This approach maintained morale while extending supplies. They also front loaded consumption of perishables while carefully rationing shelf-stable items, creating a natural transition from normal eating patterns to more restricted consumption.

Your medical supplies likely present the most critical extension challenge. Unlike food, where reduced consumption is uncomfortable but feasible, many medications cannot be safely rationed. The solution lies in aggressive conservation of non-prescription supplies combined with alternative approaches for common conditions.

For first aid supplies, implement strict usage protocols—smaller bandages than you might normally use, multiple-stage cleaning for wounds to reduce antiseptic usage, careful sterilization and reuse of items typically considered disposable. Create dedicated medical supply management with clear documentation of inventory and consumption. This prevents the common problem of supply exhaustion from casual usage that could have been addressed through alternative means.

For chronic medical conditions requiring prescription medications, the extension strategy must begin before the crisis. Work with healthcare providers to gradually build a buffer supply through slightly accelerated refill timing where legally possible. During the crisis itself, implement perfect medication compliance to maximize effectiveness—taking medications exactly as prescribed with appropriate timing, food considerations, and complementary non-pharmaceutical approaches to optimize their effectiveness.

Energy resources—batteries, fuel, alternative power—require strategic deployment planning. Establish clear usage hierarchies based on critical needs versus conveniences. Create scheduled usage windows rather than continuous operation. Implement complementary non-powered alternatives for essential functions where possible. During an extended winter power outage, I observed a family maintain critical function by operating their generator just four hours daily—two hours in the morning and two in the evening—rather than attempting continuous operation that would have exhausted their fuel supply within days.

The psychological component of resource extension cannot be overestimated. Humans adapt remarkably well to consistent restrictions but struggle with uncertainty and perceived inequity. Create clear, transparent consumption protocols that apply equally to all household members (with appropriate adjustments for medical needs, age, or special circumstances). The predictability of knowing exactly what resources are available and how they will be allocated provides crucial psychological stability during extended crisis conditions.

Resource Renewal and Replenishment Strategies

No matter how extensive your initial preparations, true long-term survival depends on transitioning from consumption to production. This shift represents perhaps the most fundamental adaptation required for extended crisis survival.

Maria's family had weathered the first two weeks after the earthquake admirably. Their stored water, food, and emergency supplies had carried them through the immediate aftermath. But as I sat with them on Day 17, reviewing their dwindling resources, the brutal mathematics of consumption without replenishment was becoming clear. Their water would last another week at most. Their food perhaps ten days. Without establishing renewal systems, they faced increasingly desperate circumstances. What followed was a case study in resourceful adaptation.

Water represents your most immediate replenishment priority. In all but the most extreme environments, multiple collection opportunities exist that become viable when conventional sources fail. Rainfall harvesting provides the most accessible option in many environments. During extended recovery operations, I've helped families implement remarkably effective collection systems using materials salvaged from their own homes—rain gutters redirected into storage containers, tarps arranged to channel water into collection points, even children's wading pools deployed as primary collectors.

The key to effective water replenishment isn't the initial collection but the integrated management system. Successful long-term adaptation requires categorizing water by source and quality, then matching usage to appropriate quality levels. Rainwater from a relatively clean collection surface can be rendered potable with minimal treatment. Groundwater from shallow collection may require more extensive purification but remains viable for multiple uses. Even grey water from previous uses can be repurposed for non-consumption applications.

Food replenishment follows a similar progression from opportunistic to systematic. In the initial transition period, focus on preserving and extending existing food resources. Implement sprouting systems for available beans, grains, and seeds—

creating living food that multiplies the nutritional value of stored dry goods while providing essential micronutrients increasingly scarce in shelf-stable foods.

As the crisis extends, transition toward deliberate production. During extended urban disruptions, I've documented families transforming decorative landscaping into productive garden space within days. The most successful approaches focus on fast-growing, high-yield crops requiring minimal care—leafy greens, radishes, green onions, bush beans. Container gardening using repurposed vessels allows production even in limited spaces. Window-sill herb gardens provide both nutritional and psychological benefits through fresh additions to increasingly monotonous diets.

Animal protein replenishment presents greater challenges but significant rewards. Small-scale egg production through backyard chickens provides exceptional return on investment for those with appropriate space. In rural and suburban settings, fishing, trapping, and hunting become viable options—though each requires specific skills, knowledge, and tools. The most consistently successful protein replenishment strategy I've observed in extended crises has been insect harvesting—particularly crickets, mealworms, and similar high-protein, easily cultivated species. While culturally unfamiliar to many Americans, these protein sources require minimal space, convert feed to protein far more efficiently than conventional livestock, and can be incorporated into existing foods in ways that overcome initial resistance.

Energy replenishment requires systematic thinking about both generation and conservation. Solar charging systems, even small-scale ones designed for camping or emergency use, can maintain critical electronics indefinitely when paired with disciplined usage protocols. Wood fuel, properly harvested and seasoned, provides sustainable heating and cooking capability in appropriate environments. Human-powered energy generation—from hand-crank systems to bicycle generators—creates critical redundancy for essential functions.

The most comprehensive resource replenishment strategy I've documented came from a family in the aftermath of a regional ice storm that left their area without power for nearly six weeks. They implemented what they called their "input-output matrix"—systematically identifying every resource they consumed, then developing at least two methods to replenish each one. Water came from rainfall collection and snow melting. Food combined stored supplies with aggressive foraging and container gardening under improvised grow lights. Energy came from solar chargers, a small wind turbine constructed from salvaged materials, and systematic collection of fallen wood processed into usable sizes. This comprehensive approach allowed them to maintain not just survival but relative comfort throughout an extended crisis that defeated many of their less-adaptive neighbors.

The transition from reliance on stored resources to active replenishment represents the most critical adaptation for long-term crisis survival. This shift is as much psychological as practical—moving from a mindset of careful conservation to one of deliberate production. Those who make this transition successfully typically describe it as empowering rather than overwhelming. Despite the challenges, they report a profound satisfaction in creating sustainability in the midst of disruption.

Psychological Adjustment to the New Normal

The most dangerous threats in extended crises often aren't external—they're internal. Even individuals with excellent

235

physical preparation can completely deteriorate psychologically, while others with minimal material resources demonstrated remarkable resilience through their mental adaptation.

Roberto had been a successful executive before the earthquake. Three weeks into the aftermath, I found him sitting in the wreckage of his luxury apartment, surrounded by high-end survival gear he'd meticulously acquired over years of preparation. Despite his physical needs being met, he was barely functional— unable to make basic decisions, alternating between rage and despair, consumed by the gap between his previous life and current reality. Two floors below, Elena—a university student with minimal supplies—had organized a community support network, empowered creative resource sharing systems, and maintained not just functionality but genuine optimism. The difference wasn't in their supplies but in their adaptability to radical change.

The psychological trajectory of extended crisis follows a predictable pattern. The initial emergency period brings heightened alertness, often accompanied by effective decision-making and action. As this phase ends—typically within the first week—many experience a profound crash. The sustained stress hormones deplete, reality sets in, and the recognition that "normal" isn't returning anytime soon creates a grieving process that can manifest as depression, anxiety, irritability, or emotional numbness.

Successfully navigating this transition requires deliberate psychological strategies. Establishing structured routines provides crucial stability when external conditions remain chaotic. During extended displacement after floods, I worked with families who implemented rigid daily schedules—set times for waking, meals, activities, and sleep. Those maintaining these structures demonstrated significantly better psychological outcomes than those who allowed their days to remain unstructured, regardless of their material circumstances.

Purposeful activity plays an equally critical role in psychological adaptation. The mind requires meaningful engagement to maintain health. In extended crises, this often means reframing necessary survival tasks as meaningful work rather than unwelcome burdens. The most psychologically resilient individuals approached their situations as challenges to be mastered rather than disasters to be endured. They took genuine pride in innovative solutions, resource optimization, and skill development—finding purpose in the very circumstances others found only deprivation.

The social dimension of psychological adaptation cannot be overstated. Humans are fundamentally social creatures, and isolation dramatically accelerates psychological deterioration. During extended disaster recovery operations, I've consistently observed better outcomes among those who established or maintained community connections. Even simple structures— daily check-ins with neighbors, scheduled community meals, collaborative work projects—provided critical social support that sustained psychological resilience.

Maintaining perspective through information management represents another key adaptation. In the absence of reliable information, humans naturally catastrophize—imagining worst-case scenarios and acting as if they're certain. During communication disruptions, I've worked with communities implementing regular "information sessions" where verified facts were clearly distinguished from speculation, rumors were addressed directly, and uncertain information was properly contextualized. This structured approach prevented the psychological deterioration that often accompanies information vacuums.

Perhaps the most powerful psychological adaptation comes through meaning-making—the human capacity to derive purpose from adversity. In crisis environments, I've interviewed hundreds of individuals about their coping strategies. Those demonstrating the greatest resilience consistently reported finding meaning beyond mere survival—protecting vulnerable community members, preserving cultural knowledge, modeling resilience for children, developing systems that might help others in future crises. This transcendent purpose provided psychological sustainability that material resources alone could never deliver.

The practical implementation of psychological adaptation requires intentional effort. Create dedicated times for emotional processing—whether through journaling, structured conversations, or other reflective practices. Implement stress management techniques appropriate to available resources—from formal meditation to simple breathing exercises. Establish celebration rituals for successes no matter how small, creating psychological momentum through acknowledged progress.

The most profound psychological adaptation I've witnessed came from Sara, a middle-aged woman who lost everything in a devastating hurricane. Six months into the recovery, while still living in temporary housing, she told me: "I finally realized I was mourning the life I'd planned while missing the life I had. Once I started fully living in this reality instead of rejecting it, I discovered strengths I never knew I possessed." This fundamental shift—from resistance to engagement—marks the difference between those who merely survive extended crises and those who find ways to thrive within them.

Skill Acquisition Priorities for Long-Term Viability

In long-term crisis situations, what you know ultimately becomes more valuable than what you have. Your supplies will eventually deplete, but your skills can both extend those supplies and create sustainable alternatives.

When I met Jason three weeks after the regional floods, he was in a desperate situation. A successful IT professional before the disaster, his technical expertise had become temporarily irrelevant in an environment without reliable electricity or internet. Despite having assembled reasonable emergency supplies, he lacked the practical skills to extend them through adversity. Our conversation that day began his crash course in crisis-relevant skill development—an education that quite literally saved his life in the weeks that followed.

The transition to long-term survival requires strategic skill acquisition focused on maximum return for your limited learning time and energy. Rather than attempting to master every possible crisis skill—an impossible task—focus on the capability categories that provide the greatest versatility and survival impact.

Water skills represent your first acquisition priority. Beyond basic purification techniques, develop capabilities in source identification, quality assessment, and advanced collection. Learning to identify groundwater indicators, construct simple filtration systems, and implement passive collection methods provides tremendous return on investment. During drought conditions following wildfires, I worked with a community that built a comprehensive water skills development program— teaching members to locate natural seeps, construct solar stills, and develop rainwater harvesting systems. This knowledge proved far more valuable than their initial stored supplies as the crisis extended from weeks into months.

Food procurement skills provide your next critical capability development. Modern Americans typically possess minimal knowledge of food sources beyond commercial systems. Developing even basic foraging capabilities dramatically extends your resource base. Focus initial learning on the most common edible plants in your specific environment, particularly those often considered "weeds" that grow abundantly without cultivation. Complementary skills in simple trapping, fishing methods appropriate to local water sources, and hunting techniques aligned with available tools create critical redundancy in protein acquisition.

The most impressive food skill development I've witnessed during a crisis came from an urban neighborhood that implemented a systematic "lawn-to-garden" transformation. Within weeks, they had converted decorative landscaping into productive growing spaces, focusing on fast-maturing crops that provided both calories and essential nutrients. Their success came not from previous gardening experience—most had none—but from disciplined skill acquisition focused on immediate application. They learned only what they needed for their next implementation step, then immediately applied that knowledge before moving to the next skill.

Medical capability development follows a similar targeted approach. Rather than attempting to become emergency physicians, focus on the conditions most likely to occur in your specific situation. Wound management, infection prevention, and non-pharmaceutical intervention for common ailments provide the highest return on learning investment. Particular focus on hygiene-related disease prevention often proves most valuable, as these conditions become increasingly common as infrastructure failure continues.

During recovery operations, I've helped with community-based medical skill development programs focusing on realistic capability targets. The most successful approaches pair knowledge acquisition with resource extension—learning to create wound care supplies from available materials, developing alternatives to commercial medications using locally available plants, and implementing preventative protocols that reduce medical needs before they develop.

Technical skills form another critical category for long-term viability. Basic repair capabilities for essential systems—water collection, shelter maintenance, tool preservation—reduce vulnerability to cascading failures. Simple mechanical knowledge, particularly regarding manual alternatives to power-dependent systems, creates crucial adaptability. Fundamental electrical understanding, especially regarding low-voltage DC systems common in alternative energy setups, enables maintaining critical functions despite infrastructure failure.

The most adaptable individuals in crises share a common approach to skill development. Rather than depth in a single area, they develop functional competence across multiple domains. They prioritize skills with wide application rather than specialized techniques. They focus on understanding principles that enable improvisation rather than memorizing specific procedures that may not fit their actual circumstances.

This adaptable approach was epitomized by Michael, a schoolteacher I worked with during recovery from a regional ice storm. With minimal prior technical experience, he systematically developed capabilities based on immediate community needs. He learned basic water filtration, then adapted those principles to create systems from available materials.   He studied fundamental electrical concepts, then applied them to maintain critical charging capabilities through improvised connections. His knowledge was never comprehensive, but it was immediately applicable and adaptable to changing circumstances.

The psychological dimension of skill acquisition deserves particular attention. Beyond the practical value of new capabilities, the process of learning itself provides powerful psychological benefits during crises. The growth mindset required for skill development counteracts the helplessness often experienced in disaster situations. The progressive mastery of new capabilities builds confidence that generalizes to other challenges. The focus required for learning provides healthy psychological distraction from circumstances that might otherwise become overwhelming.

The most effective skill acquisition method in crisis situations follows a consistent pattern: learn, apply, teach. Individuals first acquire a specific capability through any available means— observation, experimentation, guidance from knowledgeable community members, referenced materials. They immediately apply this knowledge, adapting as necessary for available resources. Finally, they teach the skill to others, which both solidifies their own understanding and creates valuable capability redundancy within their community.

This **learn-apply-teach** cycle was brilliantly implemented by a neighborhood association during extended power outages following severe storms. They established daily skill-sharing sessions where individuals who had developed specific capabilities taught others, who then practiced under guidance before teaching additional community members. This distributed learning model rapidly spread critical knowledge throughout the community while strengthening social bonds that supported psychological resilience.

Planning for Recovery or Adapting to Permanent Change

Perhaps the most challenging aspect of extended crisis management is balancing between preparing for eventual return to normal systems and adapting to potentially permanent changes. This tension manifests in nearly every decision: How much effort should you invest in temporary systems versus durable alternatives? How should you allocate limited resources between immediate needs and long-term solutions? When should you maintain connections to previous patterns versus developing entirely new approaches?

Karen faced this dilemma five weeks after the earthquake. With her apartment building condemned but still standing, she needed to decide whether to risk retrieving more of her possessions or focus entirely on establishing her new living situation. Her limited time and energy couldn't accommodate both priorities equally. The government promised utilities would be restored "soon," but similar promises had already proven hollow multiple times. Should she invest in better adaptations to the current reality or prepare for the promised recovery? Her decision process illustrates the complex navigation required in extended crises.

The balanced approach begins with tiered planning—developing strategies for different potential time frames simultaneously. Immediate adaptations address your current circumstances with available resources. Intermediate systems prepare for extended disruption while maintaining flexibility. Long-term approaches acknowledge the possibility of permanent changes while preserving options for reintegration if recovery occurs.

This tiered approach was effectively implemented by a rural community following infrastructure damage that left them isolated for nearly six months. Rather than either waiting passively for outside restoration or abandoning hope of reconnection, they developed parallel systems operating on different assumptions. They created immediate workarounds for critical needs while also establishing more durable solutions designed for potential permanence.

Their water management exemplified this balanced strategy. Initially, they relied on stored supplies supplemented by expedient collection from available sources. But they also developed intermediate systems including community-scale filtration and coordinated collection points. In parallel, they began implementing long-term solutions—rehabilitating old wells, developing spring sources, and constructing rainwater harvesting systems designed for permanent use. Each tier operated independently yet complemented the others, providing both immediate needs and future options.

Resource allocation within this tiered approach requires strategic thinking about different recovery scenarios. The most effective method uses the "minimum viable increment" concept—identifying the smallest investment that creates functional capability at each tier. Rather than fully developing any single system, this approach creates basic functionality across multiple time frames, then progressively enhances each based on emerging conditions.

This incremental method proved invaluable during flooding recovery, where infrastructure restoration timelines repeatedly shifted. Families implementing the minimum viable increment approach maintained necessary functionality regardless of whether services were restored in days, weeks, or months.

They avoided both the wasted investment of over-committing to temporary solutions and the vulnerability of waiting for permanent restoration that continually delayed.

Information management plays a crucial role in balanced recovery planning. Reliable intelligence about restoration efforts, government assistance, and community developments allows more informed decision-making about resource allocation. During long-term disaster operations, I've helped communities set up information verification systems specifically focused on recovery timelines—cross-checking official statements against observable progress, developing independent assessment methods, and creating realistic projections based on actual conditions rather than announced schedules.

These verification systems prevented both premature abandonment of temporary measures when restoration seemed imminent and dangerous reliance on promised assistance that failed to materialize. The most effective approaches maintained healthy skepticism without descending into counterproductive cynicism—a balanced perspective that acknowledged both progress and limitations in recovery efforts.

The psychological dimension of this balance deserves particular attention. Humans naturally seek certainty, making the ambiguity of crisis recovery especially challenging. The most resilient individuals develop comfort with provisional plans— approaches explicitly designed to adapt as conditions evolve. Rather than committing psychologically to a specific timeline or outcome, they maintain readiness for multiple scenarios while taking concrete action based on current realities.

This provisional planning was exemplified by a neighborhood association managing recovery from severe hurricane damage. Rather than either assuming rapid restoration or complete abandonment of previous patterns, they explicitly developed their community resources to function under various recovery scenarios. Their communications included regular "planning horizon" discussions, where they assessed developments, adjusted expectations, and modified their approach based on emerging information—all while maintaining immediate functionality regardless of future outcomes.

The social dimension of recovery planning adds another layer of complexity. Different individuals naturally gravitate toward various recovery expectations, creating potential conflict within families and communities. During recovery operations, I've facilitated "scenario alignment" discussions that explicitly acknowledge these different perspectives while developing coordination strategies that accommodate multiple viewpoints. These structured conversations prevented the faction formation that often develops between those expecting rapid return to normalcy and those preparing for longer disruption.

Perhaps the most profound aspect of this balance involves identity preservation amidst necessary adaptation. Core values, meaningful traditions, and fundamental relationships provide psychological continuity even when external circumstances change dramatically. During extended displacement following natural disasters, I've worked with communities implementing deliberate continuity practices—maintaining significant cultural observances despite radically changed conditions, preserving educational structures despite facility loss, continuing spiritual practices despite displacement from traditional gathering places.

These continuity elements provided critical psychological anchoring that supported overall adaptation. Individuals maintaining connection to their core identity demonstrated greater resilience in managing practical changes. Families preserving key traditions navigated physical displacement more success-fully. Communities maintaining cultural practices developed more effective practical adaptations to their changed circum-stances.

The most successful long-term crisis navigation I've wit-nessed came from a community recovering from devastating floods. Their approach centered on what they called "flexible stability"—maintaining unwavering commitment to core val-ues and community cohesion while demonstrating remarkable adaptability in their practical implementation. They developed systems explicitly designed to function under multiple recovery scenarios, allocated resources proportionally across different time frames, and maintained psychological openness to various potential outcomes—all while taking concrete action to address immediate needs regardless of future developments.

Their experience illustrates the fundamental truth of extended crisis management: the goal isn't perfect prediction of future conditions but rather developing sufficient adaptability to func-tion effectively regardless of which scenario unfolds. The bal-anced approach neither abandons hope for recovery nor delays necessary adaptation while waiting for restoration that may not come. It acknowledges the reality of your current situation while preserving options for multiple possible futures—the essence of true resilience in an uncertain world.

The Seven-Day Sustainability Roadmap

By the end of your first week in crisis conditions, you must transition from emergency response to sustainable operation. This structured approach guides that critical transformation across essential survival categories.

DAY 1: RESOURCE ASSESSMENT & EXTENSION

Your first step beyond the initial emergency period requires honest inventory of your current resources and strategic planning for their extension. Today you will:

1. **Conduct complete inventory of all supplies, categorized by type and projected duration**
2. **Implement strict consumption protocols for critical resources, particularly water and food**
3. **Identify highest-priority resource limitations requiring immediate attention**
4. **Develop specific extension strategies for each critical resource category**
5. **Begin information gathering regarding external resource availability and timeline**

The effectiveness of your assessment directly determines your operational runway—the time available before resource depletion forces more drastic measures. Be brutally honest rather than optimistic in your calculations. Document everything, creating visual consumption tracking when possible to maintain awareness and discipline.

DAY 2: WATER SYSTEMS DEVELOPMENT

Water represents your most immediate sustainability challenge. Today you will:

1. **Implement comprehensive water conservation protocols across all usage categories**
2. **Establish multi-source collection systems using available materials**
3. **Develop appropriate treatment capabilities for different**

water sources

4. **Create tiered water usage system matching quality to appropriate applications**
5. **Begin developing renewable water sources for long-term sustainability**

Your water system development should focus on redundancy rather than capacity—multiple smaller sources provide greater resilience than a single large supply. Prioritize reliability over convenience, even if it requires significant lifestyle adaptation. Remember: water systems determine your absolute sustainability threshold—all other adaptations become irrelevant if water needs cannot be met.

DAY 3: FOOD STRATEGY TRANSFORMATION

By your third day of transition, food sustainability requires concrete action. Today you will:

1. **Reorganize existing food supplies based on preservation needs and nutritional priorities**
2. **Implement preservation techniques for any remaining perishable foods**
3. **Establish fixed consumption protocols with clear rationing standards**
4. **Begin immediate food acquisition through appropriate methods for your environment**
5. **Initiate production capabilities through sprouting, fast-growing crops, or other methods**

Your food strategy should balance immediate consumption needs with longer-term sustainability development. The psychological impact of food security cannot be overstated—the confidence that comes from functional food systems significantly enhances your ability to address other challenges effectively.

DAY 4: ENERGY & ENVIRONMENTAL CONTROL

Sustainable energy management becomes critical by day four. Today you will:

1. Implement comprehensive energy conservation protocols across all systems
2. Establish tiered usage priorities based on critical needs versus conveniences
3. Develop alternative energy capabilities appropriate to available resources
4. Create microclimate management systems for core living spaces
5. Begin developing renewable energy systems for priority functions

Your energy strategy should focus on function rather than convenience—maintaining critical capabilities at minimal consumption levels. Remember that environmental management, particularly temperature regulation, often represents your largest energy requirement. Passive systems that require no energy input should be prioritized whenever possible.

DAY 5: SECURITY & COMMUNICATION ENHANCEMENT

By day five, security and communication systems require formalization. Today you will:

1. **Conduct thorough security assessment of your location and situation**
2. **Implement appropriate physical security measures based**

on actual threat profile
3. **Establish communication protocols within your group and with trusted others**
4. **Develop information gathering systems for situation awareness**
5. **Create operational security measures to protect critical resources and capabilities**

Your security approach should prioritize deterrence and awareness over confrontation. Effective security integrates physical measures, behavioral adaptations, and information management into a comprehensive system focused on threat prevention rather than response.

DAY 6: HEALTH & SANITATION SYSTEMS

Maintaining health requires systematic approach by day six. Today you will:

1. **Establish comprehensive sanitation protocols to prevent disease development**
2. **Implement water and food safety systems appropriate to current conditions**
3. **Develop preventative health measures for common crisis-related conditions**
4. **Create medical resource management system with clear usage priorities**
5. **Begin developing sustainable alternatives for critical medical resources**

Your health systems should emphasize prevention over treatment whenever possible. Sanitation, particularly human waste management, often represents the most critical component of

251

long-term health maintenance in extended crisis situations. Create systems that remain functional despite limited resource availability.

DAY 7: COMMUNITY INTEGRATION & LONG-TERM PLAN-NING

Your final transition day focuses on social sustainability and future development. Today you will:

1. **Assess community resources and potential cooperative relationships**
2. **Establish appropriate integration with trustworthy community members**
3. **Develop skill acquisition plan based on highest-priority capability needs**
4. **Create tiered planning framework for different potential recovery timeframes**
5. **Implement psychological sustainability practices for extended crisis conditions**

Your community approach should balance security considerations with the substantial benefits of appropriate cooperation. The most successful long-term crisis navigation typically involves selective community integration rather than either complete isolation or indiscriminate cooperation.

This seven-day transition process transforms your posture from emergency response to sustainable operation. Each component builds upon the previous day's development, creating an integrated system capable of indefinite function rather than merely extending your initial preparations. The process isn't merely about physical systems—it simultaneously develops the psychological framework and operational discipline required for long-term resilience.

The goal isn't returning to your previous normal but rather creating a new normal that functions effectively within your actual circumstances. *Real life now.* The measure of success isn't how closely your new situation resembles your pre-crisis life, but rather how effectively you can meet essential needs and maintain human dignity within radically changed conditions.

12

Conclusion: You've Made It This Far

The fact that you're reading this conclusion means something profound: you've survived. Whether you're reading these words before disaster strikes or in the chaotic aftermath of one, you represent the fundamental truth I've observed across decades of disaster response—humans are remarkably adaptable when necessity demands it.

You've absorbed the tactical knowledge in the preceding chapters: water procurement, food management, security implementation, medical response, power alternatives, evacuation protocols, community building, information verification, and long-term adaptation. But knowledge alone doesn't explain why some people navigate extended crises while others falter despite similar resources and information. There's a deeper pattern I've observed among those who not merely survive but actually thrive during disruption—a fundamental mindset that transcends specific skills or supplies.

The Transition from Reaction to Creation

The most profound transition you must now make isn't about resources or skills—it's about psychological orientation. The initial phases of emergency response are inherently reactive: responding to the disaster, addressing immediate threats, meeting baseline survival needs. This reactive stance is entirely appropriate during the first 48 hours. But continuing in reaction mode beyond this period dramatically reduces your effectiveness and significantly increases psychological strain.

Elena's story exemplifies this critical shift. When I met her three weeks after the regional floods had devastated her community, she described her mindset evolution with remarkable clarity: "The first two days, I was just reacting—trying to handle each problem as it appeared. I felt like I was drowning in challenges. Then something clicked. I realized I couldn't keep playing defense. I needed to create systems, not just solve problems."

Offense, in other words.

This transition from reactive problem-solving to proactive system-building represents the fundamental difference between short-term survival and long-term resilience. Those who make this transition successfully describe a profound psychological shift—instead of constantly responding to circumstances beyond their control, they begin actively creating their new reality within the constraints of their situation.

The practical implementation of this mindset shift manifests in several key patterns:

First, successful long-term survivors transition from addressing symptoms to resolving root causes. Rather than repeatedly solving the same problems, they create systems that prevent those problems from recurring. Instead of continually treating water from questionable sources, they develop reliable collection systems for cleaner initial sources. Rather than repeatedly addressing security concerns, they implement comprehensive deterrence that prevents most threats from materializing.

Second, they shift from scarcity thinking to regenerative thinking. Initial emergency response necessarily focuses on conserving limited resources. Sustainable adaptation focuses instead on creating renewable flows. The most resilient individuals don't just stretch their stored food—they establish production systems that generate ongoing supply. They don't merely ration their initial medical supplies—they develop alternative treatments using available resources.

Third, they move from isolated solutions to integrated systems. During initial response, addressing individual problems separately makes perfect sense. As you transition to sustainable practices, the interconnection between systems becomes increasingly important. Water, food, energy, security, and health aren't separate challenges—they're aspects of an integrated living system. Those who recognize and leverage these connections develop solutions that address multiple needs simultaneously, creating remarkable efficiency with limited resources.

The Adaptability Advantage

Throughout this book, I've emphasized practical skills and tangible resources. But the most valuable survival asset isn't something you have—it's something you are. Adaptability—the capacity to adjust effectively to changed conditions—ultimately determines long-term outcomes more reliably than any specific preparation.

Miguel's experience during prolonged civil unrest demonstrates this principle with stark clarity. A corporate executive with minimal survival training but remarkable adaptability, he navigated eighteen months of severe infrastructure disruption by constantly evolving his approach as conditions changed. "My initial plans became irrelevant within days," he told me during an interview conducted by candlelight in his improvised shelter. "What saved me wasn't what I knew coming in—it was my willingness to admit when something wasn't working and try completely different approaches."

Stay Curious, My Friend

This adaptability advantage manifests through several distinct characteristics I've observed consistently among successful crisis survivors:

The most adaptable individuals maintain intense **curiosity** despite difficult circumstances. They continuously gather information, test assumptions, and seek deeper understanding of their environment. This curiosity creates continuous improvement rather than static implementation of initial solutions. During extended power outages following ice storms, I observed how curiosity-driven experimentation led to remarkable innovations in heating, water collection, and food preservation—often developed by individuals with no prior expertise in these areas.

Adaptable survivors also demonstrate psychological flexibility—maintaining core values while readily abandoning preconceptions about how those values should be deployed. They distinguish between fundamental needs and habitual preferences. During extended displacement following hurricanes, I worked with families who maintained their essential cultural and familial practices while radically changing their implementation methods to fit their new circumstances.

Perhaps most importantly, adaptable individuals cultivate response diversity—maintaining multiple options for meeting each essential need rather than relying on single solutions, no matter how seemingly robust. This approach creates true resilience through redundancy and complementarity. If one approach fails, alternatives remain viable. During wildfire evacuations, families with diverse response options navigated changing conditions more successfully than those with more resource-intensive but less flexible plans.

The practical cultivation of adaptability begins with deliberate experimentation. Rather than seeking perfect solutions, try multiple approaches simultaneously at small scales. See what works in your specific circumstances, then scale the most effective methods. This experimental mindset prevents over-commitment to unproven approaches while rapidly identifying viable strategies for your unique situation.

Finding Meaning Beyond Survival

Survival itself provides sufficient motivation during initial emergency response. But as crisis conditions drag on, mere survival proves psychologically insufficient for most people. Those who navigate longer term disruption most successfully find meaning and purpose beyond basic needs—reasons to persist that transcend mere continuation.

Sarah's experience during extended isolation following severe storms illustrates this progression powerfully. After successfully addressing immediate survival needs for herself and her children, she described reaching a psychological inflection point: "We were safe, we had water, food, and shelter—but I felt a growing emptiness. Then I realized: surviving isn't enough. We needed purpose beyond just making it to tomorrow."

Her solution transformed both her psychological state and her practical effectiveness. She began documenting their experience, developing a hand-written guide for others facing similar circumstances. This documentation project provided structure, meaning, and future orientation during months of challenging conditions. "Recording what worked and what didn't gave purpose to our struggles," she explained. "Our difficulties became valuable if they could help others."

This pattern of finding meaning through contribution appears consistently among successful long-term crisis navigation. The most effective approaches typically involve:

Creating legacy value from current challenges. Those who document their experiences, develop improved methods, or create resources that might benefit others transform their difficulties from meaningless suffering into valuable contribution. During earthquake recovery operations, I worked with community members who systematically recorded their adaptation methods, creating instructional resources that not only helped their neighbors but provided profound psychological benefit to the creators themselves.

Protecting and transmitting cultural knowledge emerges as another powerful meaning-generator. During extended displacement following floods, I observed families who took extraordinary measures to maintain educational activities for children, preserve cultural traditions, and continue creative expression despite challenging circumstances. These efforts provided structure and purpose that transcended immediate survival concerns while preserving crucial identity elements that supported psychological resilience.

Perhaps most significantly, meaning often emerges through service to others despite personal hardship. The most psychologically resilient individuals in crisis situations typically find ways to contribute to others' welfare despite their own challenges. During hurricane recovery, I interviewed dozens of survivors about their coping strategies. Those who maintained the strongest psychological health almost universally described some form of service to others—from checking on elderly neighbors to organizing community resource sharing to teaching valuable skills to fellow survivors.

The practical cultivation of meaning begins with intentional reflection about your values independent of specific methods. What truly matters to you beyond physical survival? What contributions could you make even with limited resources? What aspects of your identity and culture provide stability amid external chaos? These questions aren't philosophical luxuries—their answers provide psychological sustainability that directly enhances your physical survival prospects.

The Unexpected Survivors

Throughout my career while documenting disaster response and recovery, I've been continuously struck by who actually survives crises versus who one might predict would survive based on conventional preparedness metrics. The pattern of "unexpected survivors" has proven so consistent that it's worth explicit examination.

When disaster preparedness discussions focus on equipment, supplies, and tactical skills, they often create an implied profile of who should theoretically navigate crises most successfully: physically strong individuals with extensive supplies, weapon proficiency, and tactical training. Yet the actual demographics of successful long-term crisis navigation rarely match this profile.

Instead, I've repeatedly documented remarkable resilience among those society often considers vulnerable—elderly individuals with deep knowledge but limited physical strength, individuals with disabilities who have developed extraordinary adaptability through daily navigation of an often-inaccessible world, immigrants who have already successfully adapted to radical life changes, and those with limited financial resources who have developed remarkable creativity in addressing challenges with minimal materials.

Isabel's story exemplifies this pattern with particular clarity. At 72, with limited mobility and modest resources, conventional preparedness thinking would have categorized her as highly vulnerable when hurricanes devastated her coastal community. Yet three months later, when I interviewed residents about successful adaptation strategies, her name kept coming up as a cherished community resource. Her lifetime of experience overcoming challenges with limited means had developed extraordinary adaptability. Her deep knowledge of traditional practices provided solutions when modern approaches failed. Her established community connections facilitated resource sharing that benefited everyone involved. She hadn't merely survived—she had become a cornerstone of community resilience.

This pattern of "unexpected survivors" reveals several crucial insights about true crisis adaptability:

Experience navigating resource constraints often provides better preparation than abundance. Those who have lived with limited means frequently develop remarkable creativity in addressing needs with minimal resources—a skill that proves far more valuable in crises than having previously had easy access to whatever was needed.

Interdependence typically produces better outcomes than self-sufficiency. Despite prepper culture's emphasis on independence, those embedded in functional social networks consistently demonstrate better crisis outcomes than isolated individuals, regardless of how well-supplied those individuals might be. The mutual assistance and psychological support provided by community connections creates resilience far beyond what individual preparation alone can achieve.

Adaptability consistently outperforms specific preparation. Those with experience adapting to changing circumstances—whether through multiple relocations, navigating disability in an often-inaccessible world, or managing variable resource availability—usually navigate novel crisis conditions more effectively than those with extensive preparation for specific scenarios that inevitably differ from actual events.

The emotional regulation developed through previous adversity provides crucial psychological resilience. Those who have already overcome significant life challenges often demonstrate remarkable emotional stability during crises. This psychological resilience allows clearer thinking, better decision-making, and more effective resource management than is typically possible for those experiencing serious adversity for the first time, regardless of their material preparation.

These insights suggest a fundamental recalibration of how we practice disaster preparation. Rather than focusing exclusively on accumulating supplies and tactical skills—though these certainly have value—true preparedness might better emerge from developing adaptability, building community connections, practicing creative problem-solving with limited resources, and cultivating the psychological resilience that comes from successfully overcoming smaller challenges.

The Path Forward

As you move beyond these pages into either preparation or actual response, remember that the most valuable preparation isn't stockpiling resources—it's developing the adaptability to function effectively regardless of what specific challenges emerge. The most crucial supplies aren't those you've stored but those you can continue to acquire or create as needs evolve. The most important skills aren't those you've mastered already but those you can rapidly develop when circumstances demand them. The unexpected survivors—those who navigate extended crises with remarkable effectiveness despite limited initial preparation—consistently demonstrate these qualities: curiosity that drives continuous learning, flexibility that enables rapid adaptation, creativity that finds solutions within constraints, and connection that transforms individual vulnerability into collective resilience.

You've made it this far—either through these pages or through actual crisis conditions. The path forward involves not merely implementing the specific techniques described throughout this book but embracing the underlying principles that enable true long-term resilience: the transition from reaction to creation, the cultivation of adaptability advantage, the discovery of meaning beyond survival, and the recognition that unexpected strengths often emerge from supposed vulnerabilities.

As you face whatever challenges lie ahead—whether the theoretical possibilities of future disruption or the immediate realities of current crisis—remember that humans have navigated extraordinary challenges throughout our existence. The skills and adaptations required for current crises aren't novel inventions but rediscoveries of capabilities our species has demonstrated throughout our history. You are the descendant of innumerable ancestors who successfully beat challenges that would seem insurmountable by contemporary standards. Their resilience lives in you, waiting to be activated by necessity. In your very DNA!

The most profound truth I've observed across decades of disaster response work is simply this: you are almost certainly more capable than you realize. When necessity demands it, humans consistently demonstrate remarkable adaptability, creativity, and resilience—often to their own surprise. This capacity doesn't require extraordinary preparation or unusual talent. It requires only the willingness to engage fully with your circumstances, adapt continuously as conditions change, and find meaning beyond mere survival.

You've made it this far. You'll make it further. The qualities that enable true resilience in extraordinary circumstances are already within you, waiting to be fully expressed when circumstances demand them. Trust this deeper capacity. It has carried our species through countless crises before. It will carry you through whatever challenges lie ahead.

Use your 48 hours wisely.

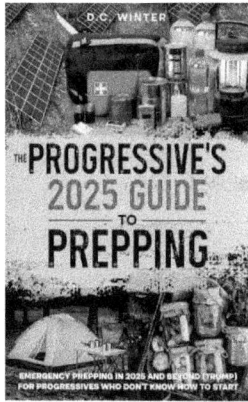

About the Author

D.C. Winter, also author of *The Progressive's 2025 Guide to Prepping*, spent over a decade as an international journalist covering climate, infrastructure, and political instability across four continents. Their perspective on preparedness was fundamentally shaped by six months in an overseas prison after being falsely accused of CIA involvement while serving in the Peace Corps – an experience that taught them firsthand how quickly systems can unravel and the importance of community resilience.

After returning to the States and witnessing the cascading crises of the early 2020s, Winter realized that reporting on problems wasn't enough. Drawing on their unique background bridging worlds – from environmental activism to emergency response, from overseas development to homesteading – they began organizing underground community resilience workshops that brought together unlikely allies across political divides.

Now based somewhere in New England, Winter divides their time between consulting on community resilience projects, teaching sustainable agriculture, and maintaining a demonstration homestead that serves as a training center for practical preparation methods. Their articles on community resilience have appeared in various environmental and progressive publications under different names.

Winter holds advanced degrees in Environmental Science and International Development, along with certificates in emergency management and permaculture design. They help coordinate several regional resilience networks while maintaining a low profile to protect the privacy of their preparation community.

Beyond their preparation work, Winter writes about the intersection of environmental justice, community resilience, and practical preparation. They live in a mostly off-grid home with their partner (an ER nurse), a flock of heritage breed chickens, and an extensive food forest that feeds both their household and their neighbors.

Winter remains deliberately vague about their exact location and identity to protect both their privacy and the network of progressive preparation communities they help support. This is their first book under this name.

Subscribe to my newsletter:

✉ https://substack.com/@wintersherepress?utm_source=user-menu

Also by D.C. Winter

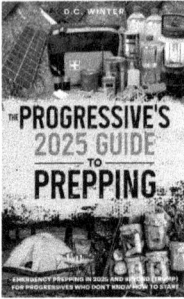

The Progressive's 2025 Guide to Prepping
Are you prepared? Welcome to turbulent 2025, when climate change isn't a debate anymore – it's your weekend forecast. As social and political unrest intensifies across communities, your concerns are justified. But what should you do as a left-leaning individual committed to positive change?

While traditional preppers retreat to their bunkers, progressives face a stark choice: compromise their values or leave their communities vulnerable. Fortunately, there's another way.

Written by former Peace Corps volunteer and environmental journalist D.C. Winter, **The Progressive's 2025 Guide to Prepping** offers a groundbreaking approach to emergency preparedness that aligns with progressive values. This isn't about stockpiling ammunition or becoming a lone wolf survivalist – it's about building sustainable community resilience for an increasingly uncertain world.

www.ingramcontent.com/pod-product-compliance
Lightning Source LLC
Chambersburg PA
CBHW060009050426
42448CB00012B/2677